Enjoy Curaçao

2024/2025

J. van Gurchom
P.C. van Mastrigt
A.A. Steevels

Good Time Concepts

Colophon

Good Time Concepts ©
Amersfoort, The Netherlands

2nd edition, 2024
ISBN: 9789492598134

Authors
J. van Gurchom
P.C. van Mastrigt
A.A. Steevels

Design
A.A. Steevels

Book layout
P.C. van Mastrigt

Photography
G.A. Johnson

Disclaimer
Although the authors and publisher have taken all reasonable care in preparing this book, we make no warranty about the accuracy or completeness of its content and, to the maximum extent permitted, disclaim all liability arising from its use.

Please send any suggestions or feedback to:
curacao@goodtimeconcepts.nl.

Bon biní na Kòrsou

Curaçao is a paradise island with a variety of possibilities for relaxation and enjoyment. Of course, you can always opt for one of the many beaches on the island, but Curaçao has much more to offer. Vacations always fly by before you know it, so this travel guide gives you a practical overview of everything you can do in Curaçao.

About this travel guide

This travel guide was written with a practical approach in mind. In addition to background information about Curaçao, you'll also find a lot of information about everything you can do on the island. From beaches, restaurants and mansions to diving locations, mountain biking and other activities. There are also a number of routes you can take that allow you to discover the most secluded spots on the island by yourself. All in all, this travel guide is compact, easy to carry, and very extensive.

Video impressions

Where pictures often say more than words, our video impressions go one step further. The short videos bring the island to life. Feel the warmth of the sun on your skin, hear the waves gently breaking on the shore and experience the unique atmosphere and versatility of Curaçao even before you leave. Scattered throughout the travel guide you will find 25 video impressions. You can recognize them by the QR codes with this icon: ▷.

How the QR codes work

QR codes are included in this travel guide. In the center of each QR code is a symbol representing what the QR code does:

⊕ These QR codes open a website with more information.

▷ These QR codes open a video.

◎ These QR codes open a route in Google Maps.

1. Find a QR code   2. Scan the QR code   3. Watch video/website

Changes and tips

In creating this travel guide, we have made every effort to update all information. If you discover on Curaçao that something in this travel guide is no longer correct, please let us know so we can adjust it for a next edition: updates@ditiscuracao.nl. If you have seen or done something on Curaçao that you think should be included in the next edition of this travel guide, we would love to hear about that too!

Independent travel guide

Good to know: all information in this travel guide has been independently compiled. None of the contributions are sponsored. Every word and recommendation are based as much as possible on our own experiences and love for Curaçao. We share the island as we experience it: pure, genuine and authentic.

Contents

NC1507
ROMAN

About Curaçao

Meet Curaçao

Ask a Curaçaoan what they think of their island and they will give a detailed eulogy about all the beautiful things the island has to offer. The colorful and cheerful shopfronts glistening in the Caribbean sun, reflect the colorful and cheerful nature of the Curaçaoan population. They are rightly proud of their paradise island and it has a relaxed atmosphere. Nobody is too busy and that's just as well. It's hot enough as it is. So sit back, relax and get to know Curaçao.

Multifaceted paradise

Of course, Curaçao revolves around the eternal sunshine, clear blue sea and white beaches. But the island has so much more to offer. Behind the swaying palm trees lies a treasure trove of diverse nature: the rugged and lush Christoffel Park in the west, the rugged seacoast in the north and the secluded areas in the northeast. Not to mention the beautiful coral reefs. The colorful underwater world of Curaçao is in the top five of many lists of favorite destinations.

Population

Curaçao has around 150,000 inhabitants. Most residents live in the capital Willemstad. There aren't any other larger 'cities' to speak of. There are some small villages and neighborhoods scattered around the island. These are purely residential areas. Unlike in Willemstad, there isn't much to do for tourists there.

Location

Curaçao is around a three hour flight from Miami and about 40 miles north of Venezuela, in the middle of the Caribbean Sea. The neighboring islands of Aruba and Bonaire are 50 and 30 miles away from Curaçao, respectively.

The ABC islands are vastly different from one another. Bonaire is pristine and quiet, Aruba is mostly 'Americanized'. Curaçao is the most authentic and largest island of the three, with its 40-miles length and average width of 6 miles. This amounts to an area of about 171 square miles.

Nationalities

It's quite remarkable then, to say the least, that Curaçao still has about 107 nationalities. This stems from the many different colonial countries that have ruled the island throughout the centuries. Most inhabitants are Creole, which is a mix of African and European. The population is the product of a troubled past in which slavery played a significant role. The slavery is still visible and tangible to this day. More on this later in the book. The Dutch, Chinese, Jews, South Americans and Surinamese have also settled here. Whatever their origin, Curaçaoans remain above all Curaçaon: friendly, smiley, relaxed and in love with their island.

Religions

Approximately 80% of the population is Roman Catholic and only 5% of the population state that they do not adhere to a particular religion. Faith, therefore, plays an important role in the life of the Curaçaoans and this is expressed, among other things, in the many churches that can be found all over the island. Yet strangely enough, there is still a shortage of churches, which means that services are regularly held in non-religious buildings.

Tourism

In addition to the local population, Curaçao welcomes around 580,000 stayover tourists annually. 43% of which are from Europe (mainly from the Netherlands), 30% from North America and 18% from South America. There are more than 710,000 day trippers visiting the island by cruise ships. This number is still increasing. Tourism is therefore one of the most important sources of income on Curaçao.
Figures refer to 2023, source: Curaçao Tourist Board.

Climate

Curaçao has a so-called 'tropical savannah climate': throughout the year the temperature doesn't drop below 28 degrees during the day and (barely) cools down at night to about 25 degrees Celsius. Maximum temperatures are between 30 degrees in the spring and 35 degrees in the autumn. The seawater also has a pleasant average temperature of about 28 degrees.

The rain season is in the fall, from October to January. This means short tropical showers and more clouds than during the rest of the year. The humidity rises in August, which can make it feel quite suffocating sometimes. However, the prevailing sun and the cooling wind fully compensate for this, making it a wonderful place to stay during this period. Curaçao is situated favorably in terms of the hurricane zone, the island rarely gets hit by hurricanes. This is also why it falls into the category of the 'Downwind Islands'.

Because Curaçao is close to the equator, it gets dark early. The sun goes down around seven in the evening and rises around the same time in the morning.

History

Curaçao has a turbulent history, which can still be seen and felt on the island today. Slavery shaped the island. There are many places spread across the entire island, where you can learn more about the history of Curaçao. Visit one of the many mansions or museums and get to know Curaçao as it once was and how it is today. This chapter explains the history of the island in a nutshell.

First residents

Curaçao was already inhabited some 4,500 years before Christ. Columbus, the explorer, described the original inhabitants as "Indians". He was under the assumption that he had arrived in India.

Curaçao was initially inhabited by the Caiquetio Indians, the Arawak Indians later also settled on Curaçao and the surrounding islands. They managed to sustain themselves with fishing and the cultivation of various natural products such as corn. Initially, these Indians lived in caves, until they settled in villages and the caves lost their function as a place to live.

While the original inhabitants of Curaçao were peaceful, around 1400 AD they were joined by some unpleasant guests: the Carib Indians who were notorious for cannibalism and their fighting skills. The Caribbean region is named after this Indian tribe.

The conquest of Curaçao

European influence

With the arrival of the Spanish conquistadors in 1499, the barbaric practices of the dreaded Carib Indians were quickly brought to an end. Spain invaded the island

and although not much was done in the first decades after the conquest, except for some cattle farming (successfully) and agriculture (very little success), in 1525 Curaçao was given its role as one of the most important slave trade centers in this region. This ushered in a dark chapter in the history of the island.

In Europe the eighty-year war broke out and the Netherlands faced a shortage of salt, while salt was badly needed to conserve fish. Salt was available in abundance in the Caribbean and the Netherlands started to play a role in this area.

West India Company (WIC)

In 1621 the West India Company (WIC) was established. Dutch 'hero of the seas' Piet Heyn performed various missions under the flag of the WIC, mostly with success. The icing on the cake was the overpowering of the Spanish silver fleet in 1628, north of Cuba. Eventually fleets of the WIC reached the Venezuelan coast. On the salt pans of Punto Araya, on the other side of Curaçao, they found their new supplier.

In the search for a defensible trade base in the Caribbean, they fell on the strategically located Curaçao which, at that time, was under the rulership of the Spanish. On 28 July 1634, a WIC expedition entered the port of Willemstad. Shortly thereafter, the Spanish surrendered and voluntarily retreated from the island, together with the original inhabitants (about 400 Arawak Indians). The capitulation of Curaçao was complete.

Defense: Fort Amsterdam

After the conquest, work began on the construction of a defensive fort. Fort Amsterdam was built on the tip of St. Anna Bay, in the Punda district. Around it a city wall was erected. The fort and the city wall formed a solid defense of the island. Today the city wall is largely demolished, but the ochre-yellow Fort Amsterdam is still in use. Now there is the Curaçao government and it serves as a governor's residence. There is also a Protestant church. The fort, the governor's residence and the church are open to the public.

To defend other points of the island against intruders, further military strongholds were built later. For example, Fort Nassau (then: Fort Republic) on the edge of the port of Willemstad and Fort Beekenburg, at the Spanish Waters. These forts can still be visited today and show clear traces from the period of the conquest.

African slave trade

In the first years after taking over Curaçao, the priority for the Dutch was to defend the island against the Spanish conquerors. When the eighty-year war came to an end, and the threat of the Spanish began to decline, the priority in Curaçao shifted from defense to slave trade.

Millions of African inhabitants were captured and brutally deported to the Caribbean. For example, they were shipped to Curaçao where they were traded: almost all slaves that were brought in were also resold. Only a handful stayed behind in Curaçao to work on the plantations.

Not only the trade in slaves was of great economic importance to the Dutch, but more and more trade in all sorts of other goods also increased. This is how Curaçao grew into an important trade center. The port of Curaçao is still the largest seaport in the Caribbean. In 1814 the slave trade was officially abolished, but slavery continued until 1863.

Origins of Willemstad

Oldest neighborhood: Punda

Willemstad consists of the Punda district (derived from Punta, which means 'point') and Otrobanda district (literally translated: 'other side'). The two districts are located on both sides of St. Anna Bay. Punda is the oldest district and was built after the completion of Fort Amsterdam. The district forms the center of Willemstad.

The houses feature characteristics of both the Dutch and Portuguese architectural style, but they are all painted in the typical Curaçao pastels. With this unique mix of styles in combination with the density of the city, Willemstad was included in the UNESCO World Heritage List in 1997.

Working class neighborhood: Otrobanda

In 1707 Punda became quite full, so Otrobanda was built on the other side of St. Anna Bay. Both Otrobanda and Punda consisted of warehouses and houses. After slavery was abolished in 1863 many Curaçaoans settled in Otrobanda as local artisans or small traders.

Chic suburb: Pietermaai

The lack of space in Punda caused the migration of wealthy, mainly Jewish, traders on the island to the Pietermaai suburb at the end of the 17th century. This district is named after ship captain, Pieter de Meij, who built three houses here. To the east of Willemstad there was a small piece of land between the sea and the Waaigat (a branch of the St. Anna Bay, see the map on page 28/29). Part of the Waaigat was drained, creating a broad foundation for the chic suburb. The rich merchants built their stately mansions here.

Villa district: Scharloo

From around 1870 onwards, a second chic suburb, called Scharloo, was built to the north of the Waaigat. A large part of the Pietermaai residents settled here after the 'orkan grandi' destroyed their homes in 1877. The villas in Scharloo were even more impressive than those in Pietermaai. The business elite spared no costs or effort and built its villas in the Renaissance style, complete with pillars, molded capitals and Spanish patios. On the cool, plant-filled patios, the rich life in Curaçao continued far into the 20th century.

Decline Pietermaai and Scharloo

Mid-20th century, residents migrated to more modern areas on the island. The wages rose and the maintenance of the villas became too expensive for the wealthy descendants. The wealthy families left their homes empty. Pietermaai and Scharloo fell into disrepair. Homeless people, addicts and prostitutes soon found shelter here. In the 1980s Pietermaai and Scharloo were refurbished house by house thanks to the active monument policy and private initiatives.

For more information about contemporary Willemstad, see page 30 and further.

Population & prosperity

Diversity

As many people visited the island throughout the last centuries and didn't leave, a very diverse population took shape. This is most apparent in the native language: Papiamento. This language originates from several African dialects, mixed with many words from Portuguese, Spanish, English and Dutch. The language was considered extremely important among the slaves at the time of the slave trade: this was the only thing that could not be taken away from them and it enabled them to communicate with each other without the slave owners being able to understand it. The current population is a melting pot of about 107 nationalities.

Isla oil refinery

When oil was found in nearby Venezuela at the beginning of the 20th century and oil production exploded in the US, Shell decided to respond by opening a refinery on Curaçao in 1918.

Prosperity

In the 1930s, 1940s and 1950s, enormous prosperity developed on the island. The oil industry provided so many jobs that many workers were brought in from surrounding areas. Partly due to automation in the oil industry, in the second half of the 20th century, those jobs disappeared as quickly as they came and Curaçao struggled with rapidly rising unemployment.

Nationalization

As a result of several oil crises, the nationalization of oil in Venezuela and the refinery's overdue maintenance, Shell decided to withdraw in 1985 and transferred the refinery to the Curaçao government for a symbolic amount of 1 guilder. This turned out to be a good deal for Shell because they made it a condition that they could never be held responsible for environmental and health damage.

Venezuelan oil company PdVSA signed a lease until 31 December 2019. Meanwhile, the refinery still accounted for 10% of the gross domestic product (GDP) and directly and indirectly employed thousands of people.

Future

In 2020, the refinery was to be acquired by the Klesch Group, but negotiations broke down under the influence of low oil prices and the corona crisis. As a result, except for maintenance work, the refinery has been completely idle since 2019. A large part of the staff was laid off.

After several failed acquisition attempts, it is still unclear whether the refinery will be put back into operation. This would be good for the island's economy, of course, but it has long been clear that the production is very harmful to public health. Consequently, the refinery is an eyesore for many.

Emergence of tourism

From the sixties onwards, the realization began to sink in that the economic model was extremely vulnerable, which became apparent in the various oil crises. Instead of focusing all the arrows on the oil industry, therefore, refuge was found in the development of various tourist activities. Curaçao has been made more accessible to tourists. In the last decade, many improvements have been made to the infrastructure, the number of hotels and other accommodation has skyrocketed and the airport has been renovated.

People are constantly trying to look ahead, but with a few very dark pages in its history and the current difficult economic circumstances, it's easier said than done. The wages on Curaçao are not bad at all in comparison to surrounding nations, but unfortunately there is still a lot of unemployment.

Tourism provides a lot of employment on Curaçao and is therefore an important source of income. The number of visitors to the island has been rising for many years now.

Kingdom of the Netherlands

Over the past decade, much has been said about the role the Netherlands plays in the Caribbean. Many say that Curaçao should become independent, while others claim that they can't survive without the support of the Netherlands.

The Netherlands Antilles were abolished on October 10th 2010. Bonaire, Saba, and St. Eustatius were renamed municipalities of the Netherlands. Curaçao and Sint Maarten have become independent countries within the Kingdom of the Netherlands, following Aruba. This means that Curaçao is no longer part of the Netherlands and is in charge, for example, of education, health care and tourism. The Netherlands remains primarily responsible for defense and foreign policy.

Culture

Although Curaçao is officially part of the Kingdom of the Netherlands, it shares very few similarities with the Netherlands: the main difference is probably the lifestyle of the local population, often characterized as relaxed and friendly. The many different nationalities form the population of Curaçao and together they have developed a unique culture over the course of centuries.

Outdoor living

The climate on Curaçao is so pleasant, it's not surprising, therefore, that people mainly live outside. There are always people out on the streets and that makes the island a wonderfully lively place to be. Particularly during the weekends, Antillean families flock to spend their free time together in the open air.

One of the places on the island to meet each other at the weekend is Caracas Bay. It is a meeting place for many families. Until late in the evening they make music and enjoy food from the grill.

Certain beaches on the west side of the island are also popular with locals at weekends, including Playa Abao (Knip). If you like crowds and are curious about the way Curaçaoans celebrate their weekend, then this beach is the place to go.

Music and dance

Music and dance are indispensable for many Curaçaoans. Beloved music and dance styles range from salsa and merengue to jazz and tumba. Tumba is one of the most important dances on the island. Although the name comes from a 17th-century Spanish dance, the tumba originally came from Africa and, under the influence of the merengue, Afro-Caribbean rhythms and jazz music, it has grown into one of the most compelling of all island dances. Today's tumba is best known for its leading role during carnival.

Carnival

The carnival on Curaçao dates back to the time of the slave trade. The rich plantation owners organized chic balls during the carnival period, where they often spend the evenings together lavishly dressed and in masks. The slaves on the plantation often celebrated a stripped-down version of this type of festival, with their own rituals and costumes. As the slaves were given more freedom and slavery was finally abolished, the workers took to the streets: the street carnival soon became more popular than the masked balls of the small elite group.

See page 134 for more information about the yearly carnival events.

Salsa, merengue en jazz

Beyond the carnival, salsa and merengue dominate the island dances. This uplifting, originally Latin-American music movement, has found many musical interpreters on the island of Curaçao. This also applies to jazz music, which is played a lot at restaurants and beach clubs.

Once on Curaçao, make sure to check the widely available Esaki-Tin events paper or check online at esaki-tin.com to see all the events taking place that week.

Food

The many nationalities and cultures here make Curaçaon cuisine extremely diverse. In most restaurants, the cuisine is international and includes most types of food, but the typical Antillean cuisine is characterized by several unique dishes, which often include fish, stewed meat and rice. This is known as 'kuminda krioyo' in Papiamento.

A great place where you can get acquainted with the authentic cuisine is the famous, covered old market: the Plasa Bieu, in the center of Willemstad (see map on page 28/29). In the beginning of the afternoon, when many locals come to enjoy their lunch, it can get very busy here.

Discover
Curaçao

AFAS
SOFTWARE

Willemstad

A.A. DE LANOOY WILLEMS BLV.
WITTE WEG
RING
JUL.
KORTIJNWEG
HOOGSTRAAT
KIJKDUINSTRAAT
ROODEWEG
BELVEDERESTRAAT
FREDERIKSTRAAT
Arubastraat
FREDERIKSTRAAT
BREEDESTRAAT
ST. ELISABETH
Hospital
LANGESTR.
KURA HULANDA VILLAGE
RIFWATERSTRAAT
Breedestraat
IJZERSTR.
KLIPSTRAAT
ST. ANNABAAI
ARUBASTRAAT
PATER EUWENSWEG
BRIONPLEIN
DE ROUVILLEWEG
FLOATING MARKET
PATER EUWENSWEG
Renaissance Mall &
Rif Fort
HANDELSKADE
JOHNNY VRUTAAL
STADIUM
BADEN POWELLWEG
Renaissance Mall &
Rif Fort
PONTJESBRUG
HEERENSTRAAT
HANCH
GOUVERNEUR VAN SLOBBEWEG
FORT AMSTERDAM
BREEDESTRAAT
GOMEZPLEIN
RENAISSANCE RIFFORT
Otrobanda
FORTPLEIN
MEGAPIER
PLASA PIAR
WATERFORTSTRA
Punda
DE BOOGJES

Willemstad

PRES. R. BETANCOURT BLV.
RING
IGIN
BRUG
BARGESTRAAT
BOLDINGSTRAAT
GOSIRAWEG
WERFSTRAAT
SCHARLOOWEG
SCHARLOOWEG
VAN DE
ANDHOFSTRAAT
Scharloo
SCHARLOOWEG
BOULEVARD ABRAHAM MENDEZ CHUMACEIRO
SYNAGOGE M.I.E.
MARSHE NOBO
PLASA MUNDO MERCED
PLASA BIEU
PRILESKADE
waaigat
OSTRAAT
AT
COLUMBUSSTRAAT
DE RUYTERKADE
CONCORDIASTRA
PRINSEN STRAAT
A. DE VEERSTRAAT
WOLKSTRAAT
DE RUYTERKADE
ANSINGHSTRAAT
WILHELMINA
PLEIN
VAN SPEYKSTR.
THEATERSTRAAT
NIEUWESTRAAT
JOHAN VAN WALBEECKPLEIN
HENDRIK
PLEIN
PIETERMAAI
PIETERMAAI
KAYA WILSON GODETT
PEN
Pietermaai

Willemstad

The capital city, which has a population of 140,000 and is also the only city on the island, forms the colorful heart of Curaçao. Behind the pastel-colored façades on St. Anna Bay lies a similarly colorful culture. A carefree local plays their guitar on a bench in the shade, a tourist strolls through the narrow shopping streets and a Curaçaon stirs large pans in the Plasa Bieu. Willemstad is a small city full of contrast. Take the time for a walk through the city and experience for yourself how these contrasts live together under the Caribbean sun.

Vibrant & colorful

Willemstad is a busy mix of cultures. Locals, tourists and students live side by side here. Where once rich merchants traded, you now have a choice of stores, restaurants and hotels. The port is dominated by huge cruise ships. Terraces sprawl out in the shadow of old warehouses. Locals sell their Curaçaon souvenirs from stalls on the side of the road. In short, Willemstad is a bustling, (mainly) tourist-oriented city. This chapter provides you with an overview of the highlights in each district.

Parking

tip!

Everywhere in Willemstad is paid parking. Therefore, park in the large free and secured parking lot Plasa Mundo Merced, at the Waaigat (see map on previous page). In minutes you walk across the pedestrian bridge into the streets of Punda.

Punda

Shopping

Shopping streets

Punda is the shopping heart of the city. In the narrow, car-free streets behind the Handelskade you can find small boutiques, electronics stores, jewelers and perfume stores. Do not expect a spectacular shopping scene here. The stores here are mainly aimed at international tourists who want to buy duty-free cameras, perfumes and jewelry. In particular the striking Penha building on the corner of the Breedestraat is an example of this: traditionally a warehouse and a house, now a department store for duty-free lifestyle products. Furthermore, most stores are located in the Heerenstraat and Madurostraat.

Marshe Nobo

Marshe Nobo is a round covered market on De Ruyterkade. Here you can shop for vegetables, fruit, fish, Curaçao "sneks" and souvenirs. Much of the same is sold here and as is the case with any other tourist market, haggling is allowed. You can visit the market at the beginning of the afternoon.

Food and drinks

Plasa Bieu

Do as the Curaçaoans do and have lunch in Plasa Bieu, the covered food hall. Plasa Bieu, sometimes also referred to as Marshe Bieu, is highly recommended for those who want to get to know the typical Curaçao cuisine (kuminda krioyo). Upon entering you are instantly met with exotic smells and scents. The hall has several operators, each with their own stall, situated along the length of the hall. Each stall offers its own specialty. When you come here for the first time, don't hesitate to have a look around, before deciding to sit somewhere. It is mainly the Curaçao women who run the kitchen. On the other side of the hall are wooden picnic tables covered with colorful tablecloths in long rows. Found a spot? Then enjoy the special fish dishes such as "bakijou" or "karko" or a "stoba" of goat. Do not forget to add the "pika" from the pots on the table: Curaçao's unique version of a spicy red sauce.

Plasa Bieu is located on De Ruyterkade and is open from Monday to Saturday, from 10am to about 3pm.

De Boogjes

De Boogjes, literally translated as 'the arches', are remnants of the old Waterfort. The Waterfort was built in 1830 as an extra defense fort. The vaulted cellars (popularly known as 'arches') served as storage cellars for ammunition, water and food. Today it houses several restaurants, with terraces overlooking the sea. De Boogjes are located on the Waterfortstraat.

For more restaurants see page 108 and further.

Attractions

Synagogue

Curaçao has the oldest synagogue (1732) in the western hemisphere that has been in continuous use. It seems remarkable, but makes sense when you consider that already since the 17th century, Curaçao has been home to a large Jewish community. The synagogue is beautiful inside. Dark mahogany furniture is in stark contrast to the white walls and copper chandeliers. The whole floor is littered with sand, which symbolizes the Jewish journey through the desert. The Mikvé Israel-Emanuel synagogue can be visited from Monday to Friday from 9 am to 4:30pm. The synagogue is located on the Hanchi Snoa in Punda.

Floating market

Around the corner from the Handelskade is the floating market: a series of small boats with Venezuelan vendors selling their vegetables, fruit and fish. The Venezuelans are far away from home and spend the night in their boats. The boats are hidden behind the stalls. When you walk a little further, you get a good view of the boats from the bridge behind the floating market.

Bridges

Punda and Otrobanda are connected by the Pontoon Bridge (officially the Queen Emma Bridge). A unique bridge construction that floats on the water by means of floating platforms (pontoons). If a ship has to pass by, the bridge will "sail" open by way of a driving engine at the end of the bridge. Pedestrians who want to cross don't have to wait, they can use the free ferry services that sail back and forth. Because the pontoons drift on the water, it feels like you are onboard a boat when you cross this bridge.

In order to efficiently manage car traffic from one side to the other, in 1974, the 183-feet high Queen Juliana Bridge was built. Large ships can easily sail through underneath the bridge. The view over Willemstad from this height is breathtaking. Unfortunately, it is not allowed to go on the bridge on foot or stand still with the car.

Otrobanda

Shopping

Breedestraat

Breedestraat is the main shopping street in Otrobanda. Local residents do their daily shopping here. No international brands or large perfumeries here, but rather typical Curaçao boutiques, hair salons and sneks (snacks), complete with painted store fronts and antique signs.

Riffort

In the 19th century, the riffort was built as an extra defense in the other corner of St. Anna Bay, opposite Fort Amsterdam. The fort wall is still (mostly) there. You can climb on top of the wall via a staircase. From the fort wall you have a beautiful view over the St. Anna Bay and the sea. The Renaissance Mall and Rif Fort are located in the Riffort, complete with resort, casino and cinema. There are also several stores, restaurants and terraces here. Here is also the memorial of the slave revolt of 1795.

De Rouvilleweg

A little further along the St. Anna Bay you'll find a row of stalls lined up at De Rouvilleweg. Buy your typical Curaçao souvenirs here or have a personal nameplate painted for the front door at home. Behind the De Rouvilleweg is the Brionplein. Not a particularly special square, but it's home to the statue of the Curaçao independence fighter Pedro Luis Brion.

Food and drinks

Snèks (snacks)

In Otrobanda, for a "pasteichi", a sandwich "karni stoba" or other Curaçao snacks, you go to a "snèk", a small eatery in the street. Do as the locals do and make a pit stop at a snèk to refuel. Fortunately they're not restricted to Otrobanda, there are various snèks scattered around the island.

Kurá Hulanda Village

Kura Hulanda means Dutch yard and is an initiative of Dutchman Jacob Gelt Dekker, who wanted to restore a part of dilapidated Otrobanda to its former glory. The Kura Hulanda Village consists of a hotel, stores, several terraces and a museum. The Kura Hulanda Museum provides an impressive glimpse into Curaçao's slavery past. See page 73 for more information.

What is special about the Kura Hulanda Village is that it still consists of original cottages that were built there in the past. The cottages have been completely restored and now serve as hotel rooms. It gives you a good idea of what it used to look like. In the evening, live music plays regularly in the little square amid the cottages.

Pietermaai and Scharloo

Pietermaai and Scharloo are, as previously described, traditionally the more upscale neighborhoods in Willemstad. The prosperous merchants built their imposing mansions here. After the decline of these districts in the 20th century, Pietermaai and Scharloo were gradually rebuilt. Today, the neighborhood improvement is still underway and many houses here have had their old elegance restored.

Shopping, eating, sleeping

Pietermaai is where you mainly come to dine, stay in one of the boutique hotels or to view the beautifully restored mansions. In the chapter Restaurants you will find more information about the different restaurants and bars in Pietermaai and Scharloo, starting on page 117.

Attractions

Take a walk through these neighborhoods in the afternoon and view the carefully restored colonial façades and murals. Here and there you'll still come across the odd dilapidated building, which gives the whole a raw edge and also shows that it is a neighborhood in development.

Walking through Willemstad
See several suggestions for exploring Willemstad on foot starting on page 62. From a guided tour to an audio tour to an escape game in Willemstad.

Beaches

Westpunt
Weg naar Westpunt
Playa Kalki
Playa Grandi
Playa Forti
Grote Knip
Kleine Knip
Playa Jeremi
Playa Lagun
CHRISTOFFEL PARK
Lagun
Jan Donker
Barber
Soto
Weg naar Santa Cruz
Tera Korá
Jan Kok
Sint Willibrordus
Jan Kok Baai
Grote Berg
Bullenbaai
Weg naar Westpunt
Weg naar
Cas Abao
PortoMari
Daaibooi
Kokomo Beach
(Vaersenbaai)

Map
Beaches

HATO AIRPORT
Franklin D. Rooseveltweg
aar Westpunt
Winston Churchillweg
Bonamweg
Gosieweg
Brievengat
Ring
Weg naar Santa Catarina
Santa
Catarina
Sint Jorisbaai
Ring
Santa Rosaweg
Santa
Rosa
Seru Loraweg
Sint
Michiel
Piscaderabaai
WILLEMSTAD
Schottegat
Weg naar Fuik
Caracasbaaiweg
Piscadera
Ring
Saliña
Lagun
Jan Thiel
Spaanse
Water
Oostpunt
uwbaai
Otrobanda
Punda
Pietermaai
Jan Thiel
Santa
Barbara
Caracasbaai
Piscadera Beach
Blue Bay
Marie Pampoen
Mambo Beach
Jan Thiel Beach

Beaches

The beaches of Curaçao are of the finest white sand, clear blue bays, where schools of brightly colored fish pass by the snorkelers. But no beach is like the next. The beaches differ from each other in terms of atmosphere and facilities. This travel guide gives you a complete overview of the range of beaches at all times, divided into three areas: beaches in the west, middle and east of Curaçao. Experience for yourself how relaxing life can be on the many paradise beaches.

Good to know

Some beaches are accessible and free of charge, on some of the other beaches you have to pay. Sometimes a beach bed is included in the entrance fee, elsewhere you pay for it separately. Prices range from USD 3 to USD 6 (NAF 5 to NAF 10) per person for access and the same for beach beds. The prices change regularly. We therefore don't mention specific prices per beach, just whether or not you have to pay for it.

Index

We use the following icons to display the information and facilities per beach.

 Paid access

 Showers available

 Sun loungers available

 Toilets available

 Restaurant/bar available

Beaches in the west

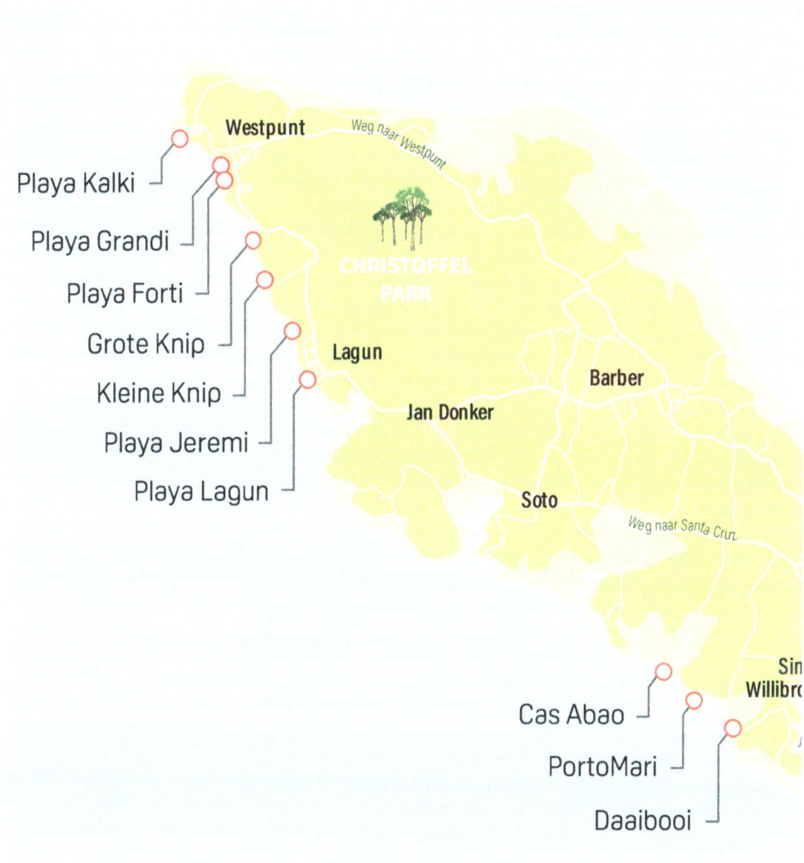

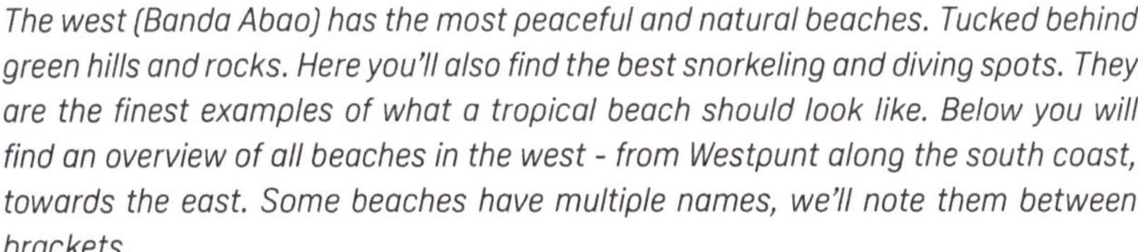

The west (Banda Abao) has the most peaceful and natural beaches. Tucked behind green hills and rocks. Here you'll also find the best snorkeling and diving spots. They are the finest examples of what a tropical beach should look like. Below you will find an overview of all beaches in the west - from Westpunt along the south coast, towards the east. Some beaches have multiple names, we'll note them between brackets.

Playa Kalki

Playa Kalki is the westernmost beach on Curaçao and owes its name to the limestone cliffs that surround the beach. The bay has one of the most beautiful reefs on the island and is therefore very popular with avid snorkelers and divers. With a bit of luck you can spot a sea turtle here. At the top-end of the beach on the cliff is the Kurá Hulanda resort. From the resort you have a beautiful view of the bay and the Caribbean Sea. Also a great place to enjoy a big lunch.

Playa Grandi (Pl. Westpunt/Piskado)

The sand is a bit coarser, dotted with loose stones and some occasional small rock formations. Playa Grandi is mainly a place for snorkeling and encountering sea turtles. On the beach, fishermen are cleaning their freshly caught fish. They toss the remains of the fish into the sea, which attract turtles. Around the pier, you can swim among them, but do not touch. There are Machineel trees on the beach that provide some shade. Additionally, there is a small snack bar and several souvenir stands.

Playa Forti

Playa Forti is a small beach with dark sand and loose stones. The beach is quiet and without any services. Playa Forti particularly attracts adventurers who dare to jump from the adjacent 40-feet high cliff. Entirely at your own risk, but refreshing and, above all, exciting. You can eat local cuisine at the restaurant on the cliff while enjoying a breath taking view of the coast line.

Grote Knip (Playa Abao)

Playa Abao (or Grote Knip) is one of the most popular beaches for both locals and tourists (especially during the weekends). It is situated in a sheltered, green bay, with high cliffs on both sides. The fine sand is bright white and the beach slowly descends into the calm and crystal clear water. It's a nice place to go snorkeling, around the cliffs. For the experienced swimmer there is a beautiful reef a little further into the sea, but watch out for boats and jet skis that may sail into the bay.

Kleine Knip (Kenepa Chiki)

Next to Grote Knip is Kleine Knip (or Playa Kenepa Chiki). Kleine Knip is literally the little brother of Grote Knip. You can go snorkeling along the rocks and there is a beautiful reef further up into the sea. There are a few more stones on the beach and a lot of washed up coral. Water booties can therefore be useful. The beach offers very little in terms of facilities and is often a lot quieter than Grote Knip.

Playa Jeremi

If you really want to escape the crowds and immerse yourself in the nature, Playa Jeremi is the place to go. There are no facilities on this hidden beach and there is only one parasol. The beach is a bit rougher, the water is crystal clear. It is also an ideal diving and snorkeling spot. Even within the bay you can regularly spot turtles. Playa Jeremi is the place to let the unspoiled nature of Curaçao really soak in.

Playa Lagún

Playa Lagún is situated in a deep cove with high rocks on both sides. The sea in the bay is therefore calm. The beach gradually declines and there are a number of stone formations on the bottom. You'll also encounter the occasional fishing boat on the beach and some palapas for shade. This gives the whole image an idyllic appearance. Playa Lagún is relatively quiet, although it has been discovered by more and more people in recent years.

Cas Abao

Cas Abao is in many a top 3 list. The fine sand here is whiter than white and the calm water is clear blue. The bay is elongated and the beach gently slopes into the sea. The many palms provide shade. The underwater world is also particularly beautiful here, even manta rays can sometimes be seen. Furthermore, there are plenty of facilities: you can have a massage on the beach or go kayaking in the bay. Note: the access road is in bad condition. You pay a fee for each car and sun lounger.

PortoMari

PortoMari is a real evergreen: the bay is long with fine, white sand and the calm sea is crystal clear here. The beach is nicely sheltered behind a row of green bushes and trees that provide plenty of shade. The restaurant has an extensive but simple menu and cozy beach bar. A reef has been laid out in the water in the form of reef balls, which attract an array of fish. PortoMari is beautiful and comfortable and can therefore get very busy. For a good spot in the shade it is best to get there early.

Daaibooi

Daaibooi is one of our personal favorites. The beach is deep and spacious and is sheltered between high rocks. It's a good place to go snorkeling along the rocks. There are some palapas and palms here for shade. Tips: make sure to drink a "coffee Kees" here, the owner's special. Or go barbecuing, which is allowed here. Daaibooi is a real family beach, a lovely place to meet at the weekend. Tip: walk up over the rocks and enjoy the beautiful view over the bay.

Beaches in central Curaçao

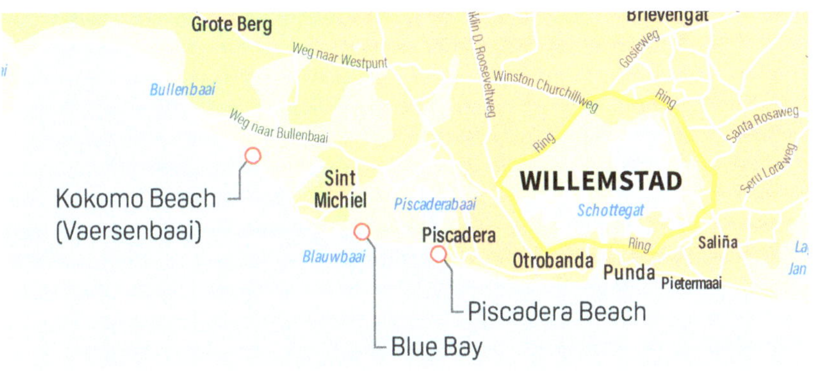

This region is located just west of Willemstad. There are three famous beaches in this area, which are fully equipped in terms of facilities. That makes these beaches especially attractive among tourists. In particular at the weekend, it can be busy.

Kokomo Beach (Vaersenbaai)

In 2011, the owner at Kokomo Beach completely renovated the formerly dilapidated Vaersenbaai and started a beach spot, complete with beach beds, palms and tarps for shade. In the weekends you have live bands and parties. On Sundays it is happy hour from 5pm to 6pm. You can not bring your own food and drink here on the beach, but there's plenty available to order. The coastline is quite rocky, but in the water around the corner is a beautiful reef.

Blue Bay

Blue Bay (or Blauwbaai) is part of the Blue Bay Resort but is accessible to everyone. The spacious beach includes private cultivated palms and large umbrellas for shade. The beach bar has an extensive snack menu which can be served on the beach. You can also dine extensively on the beach (make sure to have appropriate clothing). At the white cottage in the back you can get a massage. Every Friday there is live music during happy hour between 5pm and 7pm. There's a nice playground for children.

Piscadera Beach

The beach restaurant at Pirate Bay has a nice intimate atmosphere and has excellent international cuisine. The interior is reminiscent of a film set from Pirates of the Caribbean. The beach itself is quite small. Pirate Bay regularly organizes live performances, dance workshops, salsa evenings and a daily happy hour from 5pm to 6pm. This is also a popular wedding location.

Beaches in the east

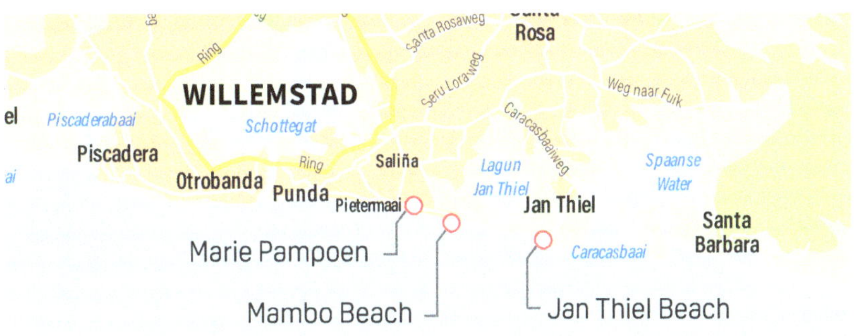

This region is located just east of Willemstad. The eastern beaches are the most touristy beaches, laid out and maintained by different beach clubs and resorts, all except for the small city beach Marie Pampoen. Although there are no idyllic bays and hidden beaches, there are many facilities that make a day at the beach very comfortable and relaxing.

Marie Pampoen

A small city beach just east of Willemstad, not suited for hours of sun bathing but you can stop here to take a refreshing dip. Locals get together here, mostly at weekends and in the evening. There's a reef which consists of old-timer car wrecks, which have been sunk to create an artificial reef. Two small diving schools are located here. Highly recommended is the Sea Side Terrace, a simple restaurant which serves local cuisine and fresh and locally caught fish (see page 120).

Mambo Beach

There's lots to enjoy throughout the day here on (and surrounding) this busy beach. Along the beach is Mambo Beach Boulevard, a recently opened shopping mall complete with stores, restaurants and bars. In the water a dam of rocks will keep the waves out, which makes it very convenient for families with little children. On the beach you will find several beach clubs side by side. Especially during the weekend, you can take advantage of the many happy hours on offer, see page 128.

Jan Thiel Beach

A popular beach with all imaginable facilities like restaurants, beach clubs, a spa to get a massage or pedicure and a diving school. If you dare you can try flyboarding, or just enjoy this spectacular water sport from the beach. Beach club Zanzibar is very pleasant during the weekly happy hour on Saturday. The beach is about 5 feet above the sea, like a kind of quay. On the sides the beach runs directly into the water. Various vacation resorts are near this bay.

Attractions

Westpunt
Weg naar Westpunt
Christoffel Park
Lagun
Jan Donker
Barber
Soto
Weg naar Santa Cruz
Tera Korá
Jan Kok
Sint Willibrordus
Jan Kok Baai
Grote Berg
Bullenbaai
Weg naar Westpunt
Weg naar Bullenbaai
HATO
Weg naar Westp
Sint Michiel
Blauwbaai

Map

Attractions

1. Christoffel Park
2. Shete Boka Park
3. Bluebay Golf
4. Old Quarry Golf
5. Curaçao Golf & Squash Club
6. Wannabike
7. Dasia
8. Surfspot Curaçao
9. Playa Kanoa
10. Kitesurfing St. Jorisbaai (Nix, Awasalu, Gusty Kiting)
11. Zapata Flyboarding
12. Sea Aquarium Park Curaçao
13. Ostrich Farm
14. Hato Caves
15. Kura Hulanda Museum
16. Savonet Museum (Christoffel park)
17. Tula Museum (Landhuis Knip)
18. The Curaçaosch Museum
19. Maritime Museum
20. Jewish Culture Historical Museum
21. Kunuku House
22. Landhuis Brakkeput MeiMei
23. Landhuis Dokterstuin
24. Landhuis Chobolobo
25. Nena Sanchez
26. Chichi Curaçao
27. Alma Blou Gallery
28. Tiki Boats Rental

Attractions

When it's time for action, Curaçao has more than enough to offer. For example, take the 1200-feet-high climb to the top of the Christoffel Mountain or go on jeep safari through the rugged west of Curaçao. Find out more about Curaçao's past and plan a route along the imposing mansions. Prefer the water? Bounce along at a speed of 60 mph across the sea with a powerboat or go windsurfing on the Spanish waters. With this travel guide you have a complete overview of all things to see or do on the island.

Walking

Interested in an adventurous hike or a leisurely stroll through the historic streets of Willemstad? Allow us to provide you with some suggestions for exploring the versatality of Curaçao on foot.

Hiking in nature

The landscape on Curaçao is ideal for hiking. There are many signposted hiking trails (about 40) that can be found all over the island. A large portion of the walking routes has been mapped out by Stichting Uniek Curaçao. On uniekcuracao.com/producten/kaarten you can download some of these maps for free. You can discover these walks on your own or join an organized tour. The landscape on Curaçao is quite accessible. The vegetation is very diverse and consists of much more than sand flats and cacti.

Below are some tips from experienced hikers on Curaçao:
• Do not go alone, find one or more people or go out with an experienced hiker. An experienced hiker knows all the corners of the island and can show you the most beautiful places.
• Protect yourself from the sun and the heat with a hat and sunscreen. Wear sturdy shoes, some paths are rocky.
• Take enough water with you.
• The ideal time for hiking is in the early morning from 7am.

- Handy to take with you: a cane and a flashlight, for caves and when the hike runs into the evening and it starts to get dark.
- Try to be back before dark.
- Never touch the fruits and leaves of a manzanilla tree. They are extremely toxic.
- The best time for a hike is early in the morning, from 7am of late in the afternoon, from 4pm.
- On birdwatchingcuracao.com you will find information on and pictures of different birds living on Curaçao.

Book a guided hiking tour

Do you want to discover all the beautiful nature Curaçao has to offer? Book a guided hiking tour with *Ingrid Hiking Tours Curaçao*. Check her Facebook-page or book a tour directly online at www.naarcuracao.com/tour-item/ingrid-hiking-tours.

Christoffel Park

The national park Christoffel Park is a must during your stay on Curaçao. Many different tropical plant and animal species can be found here. Think of colorful birdlife, deer and lizards and wild orchids, cacti and local tree species, such as dividivis and acacias. The *CARMABI Foundation* is committed to maintaining and protecting this beautiful stretch of nature. The foundation provides all sorts of activities to explore the park.

Walking trails

The park offers eight hiking routes, varying in length and difficulty. You can explore this on your own or book a guide. A guide is experienced in spotting wild animals and they can tell you stories and facts that only the locals know about. At the entrance, in the store, you can get a map that shows the routes and information about the flora, fauna and historical locations in the park.

Climb the Christoffel Mountain

The steep climb to the top of the 1200-feet-high Christoffel Mountain is perhaps the most extraordinary hike on Curaçao. Every fit person can join this climb, provided you can handle the enormous heights and steep cliffs. The route goes across sandy and rocky paths and over tree stumps. But the view on top of the summit is more than worth the adventurous climb. Especially when the sky is clear, you can look over the entire island and the endless Caribbean Sea that stretches beyond.

It's a good idea to start the climb before 9am. Due to the heat and intensity of the climb, departure later than 10am is not allowed. Do not forget to exchange your flip flops for sturdy shoes and bring enough water.

Christoffel Park
Open: Daily 6am - 2pm (entrance till 1:30pm)
Address: Entrance to the park at Savonet z/n (along the Weg naar Westpunt)
Price: Adults NAF 25.-, children from 6-12 years NAF 8.75
Christoffelpark.org | +599 9 520 1685

Shete Boka Park

Right next to Christoffel Park, on the northwest coast of the island is the Shete Boka Park. Literally translated, 'shete boka' means 'seven inlets'. This national park was established in 1994 and is also protected by the CARMABI foundation. On the Weg naar Westpunt, towards Westpunt, and past the Christoffel Park you'll find the entrance to Shete Boka Park. Do not expect green, lush hills, but rather a rugged lunar landscape, where the winds are a bit stronger and the sea hits the shoreline. This coastline contains the seven deep inlets.

Cave and breeding ground

From inland it's not that noticeable, but when you walk down the stone stairs at Boka Tabla (the centrally located boka in the extension of the parking lot) and enter the cave, the waves rush in and hit the rocks. In normal weather conditions it is safe to enter the cave, but it's always at your own risk. There is also a warning sign. Fun fact: The bokas are a protected breeding ground for sea turtles. Unfortunately these are not visible during a walk along the bokas.

Hikes

You can drive along the coastline by car and visit all bokas. If you have more time, you can explore (parts of) the park on foot. There are two walking trails:

1. A one-hour walk to Boka Wandomi. Boka Wandomi is a natural bridge that has been carved into the rocks by the water.

2. A one-hour walk that leads past Boka Brown (one of the breeding grounds for sea turtles) and Boka Pistol, the boka where the water hits the cove at its most powerful. The boka pushes up the water explosively, which sounds like a gunshot.

When hiking, keep in mind that there is no shade in the Shete Boka Park. The strong wind means you also notice the bright sun less. So make sure to put on plenty of sunscreen. A hat or scarf to cover your head is also not a bad idea here. Finally, wearing sturdy shoes is also recommended. The landscape gets quite rocky.

Shete Boka Park
Open: Daily 9am - 4:30pm | Address: Weg naar Westpunt z/n
Price: Adults: NAF 25.75, children from 6-12 years NAF 3.50,-
Shetebokapark.org | +599 9 864 0444

Walking through Willemstad

Willemstad's historic center was included on the Unesco World Heritage List in 1997 for good reason. Colonial architecture, pastel-colored merchant houses and impressive murals invite discovery while strolling through Willemstad. You can, of course, wander through Willemstad on your own, but a guided walking tour has much added value.

Guided city walks

Dushi Walks organizes various city walks in the districts of Punda, Otrobanda and Scharloo. You'll learn more about the city and its architecture and discover places you wouldn't easily visit as a tourist. Nice to know: a portion of the proceeds will be spent on all kinds of basic necessities for poor families and for the city's homeless people.

Dushi Walks Curaçao
For walking routes and bookings, see: www.dushi-walks.com
Walks take place on Mondays through Saturdays between 8:30am and 4pm

Audiotour Otrobanda

If you want to explore Otrobanda on your own, but still get some of the history and the most special places, then a "Pocketguide" audio tour might be of interest. For approximately $8.50, you can buy a voucher online to take this tour via the special app. For more information, go to www.pocketguideaudiotours.com.

Escape Game Curaçao

If you want to discover Punda and Otrobanda in a playful way, Escape Game Curaçao might be for you. At escapegamecuracao.com/en, you can purchase an access code for the app. In the app, you get several puzzles that lead you through Punda or Otrobanda. You will get to see some great places in about an hour and a half and also learn a thing or two about Willemstad.

Golfing

A popular sport on Curaçao is golf. There are several golf courses on the island:

Blue Bay Beach & Golf Resort

You can play the 18 holes on this course without a membership. It's also possible to improve your skills at any level, through a training course in the sport of golf or a separate lesson. This golf course is challenging for every level and has a beautiful location with a view of the sea.

Blue Bay Golf
www.bluebay-curacao.com/nl/activities/golf | +599 9 888 8800 (ext. 301)

Old Quarry Golf Course

According to the golf connoisseurs it's a gem among golf courses. The course was designed by the well-known golf course architect Pete Dye and is part of the chic Santa Barbara Beach & Golf Resort in the east of Curaçao. The course consists of 18 holes and gives a nice view over the Caribbean Sea and the Spanish Water. *USA Today* awarded this golf course as the best golf course in the Caribbean in 2018 and 2019.

Old Quarry Golf Course
www.oldquarrygolfcuracao.com | +599 9 840 6886

Curaçao Golf & Squash Club

Also an 18-hole golf course, located next to the oil refinery in Willemstad. Not the most beautiful location of the three, but central and surrounded by greenery, exotic birds and iguanas.

Curaçao Golf & Squash Club
www.curacaogolf.com | +599 9 737 3590

Mountain biking

Mountain biking is very popular on the island. There are at least 180 miles of sign-posted cycling routes that have been set out for both beginners and advanced cyclists. You can discover these routes independently or with a guide. For those who don't want to miss anything, a guided tour is recommended. You'll come across places that are inaccessible by car, including the rugged coastline or the sandy roads that run over the old plantations. Or you can take a route along the ancient forts, through mangrove forests and along secluded beaches. Along the way there are many exotic birds and other animals to spot. Below are some addresses where you can book tours and rent bikes.

For a guided tour, go to WannaBike Curaçao
Address: Caracasbaaiweg 340, Hofi Granville
www.wannabike.com | +599 9 527 3720

The biggest rental store for mountain bikes and racing bikes is Dasia Curaçao
Open: Mon - Fri 10am - 6pm / Sat 10am - 5pm
Address: Specialized Concept Store, Kaya Flamboyan 1a, Curaçao
www.dasiacuracao.com | info@dasiacuracao.com | +599 9 737 1112

Tips

Keep the following tips in mind for a carefree trip: you're obliged to wear a helmet while cycling on Curaçao. It is highly recommended to go early in the morning or in the afternoon, when the temperatures are the most pleasant. When you are out all day long you can, for example, cycle to a beach in the morning, spend the afternoon there and go back in the afternoon. Make sure you are back before dark, take enough food and drinks with you and don't forget your sunscreen.

Water sports

A tropical island is of course the perfect place to practice all kinds of water sports. Every imaginable water sport is represented here.

Windsurfing

Curaçao has good spots for windsurfing, including the Spanish Water and Sint Jorisbaai. Surfspot Curaçao is located at the Spanish Water. You can rent equipment and take lessons, where fast results are guaranteed: you'll be able to stand on your board within the hour. The Spanish Water involves relatively calm inland water where there are virtually no waves. It is on the southeast coast of the island. Sint Jorisbaai is also an inland waterway and is on the northeast coast of the island. Here the winds are a bit stronger than at the Spanish Water.

Surfspot Curaçao
Open: Daily 10am - 6pm
Address: Caracasbaaiweg (turn left on the roundabout at the end of the road)
www.surfspotcuracao.com | +599 9 738 0883

Wave surfing

Wave surfing isn't that big on Curaçao. There are two spots where you can venture to the waves. Playa Kanoa on the rugged north coast is a good surf spot. The ever-present trade winds ensure good waves. A disadvantage is that Playa Kanoa has a reef break instead of a beach break. The coastline isn't a sandy beach, but a reef. Coral is sharp and it's easy to injure yourself. Some experience and alertness are therefore required. Playa Kanoa is an ideal surf spot for the experienced and adventurous surfer. Equipment can be rented on the beach and you can take lessons.

There are also surf spots on the coast of Klein Curaçao. But the weather and water conditions are not always ideal here.

Kitesurfing

Especially for beginners, Sint Jorisbaai is an ideal kitesurfing spot. The water is quiet and there is always a strong wind, especially in the months between February and August. Klein Curaçao is a nice spot for experienced kite surfers. The waves are much higher here and there are side winds. In addition, you can also go kitesurfing at the Marriott resort located next to the Piscadera Bay, at the beach of Marie Pampoen and at the Spanish Water.

For lessons in Sint Joris Bay:
Nix Kite School & Awa Salu Kiteboarding & Gusty Kiting
www.nixkitecuracao.com | +599 9 520 2562 | nixkitecuracao@gmail.com
awasalu-kiteboarding.com | + 599 9 562 2022 | info@awasalu-kiteboarding.com
gustykiting.com | +599 9 667 4403 | info@gustykiting.com

Flyboarding

An increasingly popular sport is flyboarding. Flyboarding is best described as 'hovering' above water with a board with hoses connected to it. These hoses allow you to build up water pressure by 'accelerating'. The power of the water makes you float above the water. The water power is driven by a kind of jetski (a 'waverunner'). If you hover above the water, it is important to keep your balance to keep 'flying'. But according to Zapata you can get the hang of it in no time. Flyboarding can be done by everyone of 14 years and older and a maximum weight of 220 lbs (100 kg).

Zapata Flyboard Caribbean
Open: Daily 10am - 5pm | Address: Jan Thielbaai beach
+599 9 512 3359 | flyboardcuracao@gmail.com

Supboarding

Another fast-growing water sport is supboarding, or Stand Up Paddling. Stand on a surfboard and paddle along using an oar. Apparently it's good for your 'core' muscles, because you're constantly using them while paddling. Supboarding can also be done at an easier level: Simply go a little slower or sit on your board. You can follow an introductory lesson, book organized tours or rent equipment at Surfspot Curaçao at the Spanish Water.

Animals

Many animals live in the wild in Curaçao, such as (predatory) birds, flamingos, deer and iguanas. Curaçao is also rich with underwater fauna, with reef fish, turtles, rays and dolphins. Wildlife spotting is great at the Christoffel Park. If you want to get real close to dolphins, sharks or even ostriches it's probably worth a visit to the Sea Aquarium Park Curaçao of the Curaçao Ostrich Farm.

Sea Aquarium Park Curaçao

Adjacent to Mambo Beach Boulevard is Sea Aquarium Park Curaçao, consisting of several sections all dedicated to Curaçao's marine life.

Curaçao Sea Aquarium

Bordering Mambo Beach Boulevard is the Sea Aquarium Park Curaçao, which consists of several parts. One of them is the Curaçao Sea Aquarium, an 'aquarium park' with 46 different aquariums. These are constantly supplied with fresh seawater using a unique open system. The Sea Aquarium houses all kinds of reef fish and predators, such as stingrays and sharks.

In the outdoor area there are several lagoons with sea turtles, sea lions, sharks, stingrays and dolphins. Educational sessions are regularly held here with sea lions and dolphins. The dolphin demonstration in particular is a very popular feature here. The Curaçao Sea Aquarium regularly provides care and shelter for injured or rejected animals

Animal Encounters

At the adjacent diving school, Ocean Encounters, you can book a so-called 'Animal Encounter' where you can view several sea animals up close. Equipped with snorkeling or diving equipment you can view and feed sharks, stingrays and other large fish in one of the Curaçao Sea Aquarium's lagoons. Access to the Sea Aquarium Park is included in an animal encounter.

Dolphin Academy

At Dolphin Academy you can swim with dolphins. There are several 'encounters' available to book: from touching dolphins in a basin to snorkeling and diving with dolphins in the open sea. It is advisable to book an 'encounter' in time. For more information, visit dolphin-academy.com.

Curaçao Dolphin Therapy and Research Centre (C.D.T.C.)

The CDTC offers a unique and effective therapy program for people suffering from, for example, autism, Down syndrome and mental illnesses such as depression, PTSD and burnout. This is provided by qualified therapists in collaboration with dolphins, in an inviting Caribbean environment. For more information, visit the website of Curaçao Dolphin Therapy center, cdtc.info.

Sea Aquarium Park Curaçao
Open: Tue - Sat: 8am - 5pm | Address: Bapor Kibra z/n (at the end of Mambo Beach)
Price: Adults: $ 15.-, Children 5 - 12 years $ 7.-, <5 years free entrance
www.curacao-sea-aquarium.com | +599 9 461 6666

Curaçao Ostrich Farm

A special initiative on the island is the Ostrich Farm. Once established as an export site where the eggs, chicks and meat of ostriches were exported to countries in South America. Since 1995, the farm has been open to visitors and there are several excursions you can book, you can eat ostrich steak in Zambezi restaurant and buy African souvenirs in the souvenir store.

Safari tour

The only way to see the animals from nearby is by booking a safari tour. With a semi open bus you make a 45 minutes tour of the terrain and an enthusiastic guide will tell you lots about the life of the ostriches on the farm. This is accompanied by interactions with the ostriches: you can feed the birds, touch eggs to feel their hard shell and with a bit of luck hold an ostrich chick just hatched from the egg.

Restaurant Zambezi

Before or after the tour it's great to just sit back and relax on the porch at the Zambezi restaurant. The menu includes a mix of international and Curaçaon cuisine with an African twist. In addition, Zambezi – as expected - serves a number of dishes containing ostrich meat. The ostrich steak is a must. Dining is only possible on Fridays, but you must reserve.

Curaçao Ostrich Farm & Restaurant Zambezi
Open: Daily 9am - 4:30pm, tours Daily 9am - 4pm (starting each hour)
Address: Groot St. Joris West z/n | Price: Adults $ 20.-, Children $ 15.-
www.curacaoostrichfarm.com | +599 9 747 2777

Exploring culture

Curaçao offers a wide range of museums, mansions and even caves which tell you something about the culture and history of the island. A number of old plantation houses have been converted into museums. But there are also art galleries, a Jewish museum and the Maritime Museum. In short, Curaçao also has plenty to offer when it comes to cultural attractions.

Hato caves

Near the airport are the Hato caves. Remains of Curaçao's first civilization, the Arawak Indians, can be found here. They lived in these caves. The mural drawings that are still vaguely visible are proof of this. In addition, skeletons have been found of these first inhabitants.

Many centuries later, slaves fled to these caves to hide from their slave drivers. The burning torches left visible traces of soot in the caves. Nowadays the caves are inhabited by bats.

The caves can be visited during a tour with a guide. The guide will lead you through the different 'rooms' with impressive stalactite formations and tell you about the history of the caves.

Hato caves

Open: Daily 9am - 3pm | Multilingual tours start every hour, final tour starts at 3pm (tour is compulsory) | Address: F.D. Rooseveltweg z/n | Price: Adults NAF 15,75, Children 4 - 11 years NAF 12.25
Curacaohatocaves.com

Museums

Kurá Hulanda Museum

This is the museum to go to in Curaçao when you want to learn more about the turbulent period that involved the slave trade between the Netherlands and Curaçao. The Kurà Hulanda Museum is an anthropological museum that gives a detailed picture of what happened to Curaçao during the time of slavery. In addition, the museum houses an extensive collection of African and Antillean (religious) art.

The museum is located in the middle of the Kurà Hulanda Village. This site has been completely restored to its original state. The old laborer's houses have been converted into hotel rooms and arranged in a picturesque manner around a courtyard, where you'll regularly hear live music being played. After a visit to the museum you can also enjoy a great lunch here. In order to better understand the history and contemporary life of Curaçao and the Caribbean, this museum is an absolute *must*.

Kurá Hulanda Museum

Mon - Sat 8am - 4pm, Sun 8am - 2pm | Address: Klipstraat 9, Otrobanda
Price: Adults NAF 22.-, Children till 12 years NAF 12.50
www.kurahulandavillage.com/place/museum-kura-hulanda | +599 9 462 9737

Savonet museum

In the heart of Christoffel Park is the former Savonet Plantation. The mansion and outbuildings have been completely restored and converted into a museum. The museum provides insight into the history of the park and its inhabitants. From the life of the Arawak Indians who lived here 4,000 years ago, to life during the slavery period, ending with life in the park today. Both the cultural and natural developments in the park are highlighted. For recent admission prices go to Savonetmuseum.org.

Savonet museum
Open: Daily 6am - 2pm | Address: Weg naar Westpunt (entrance Christoffel Park)
Price: Adults & children > 6 years $3.-

Tula Museum (Landhuis Knip)

Perched on top of the green hills to the west is 'Landhuis Knip' (Knip Mansion), also known as Kenepa, named after the fruit from the kenepa tree. It was once one of the most prosperous mansions, Dividivi seed pots and sheep wool were produced here. Knip Mansion is not only worth a visit for its location, but also for its history. On 17 August 1795, the largest slave revolt of the Caribbean started here.

Led by Tula, a few of the more than 350 slaves who worked at Knip refused to work. They moved eastwards across the island and more and more slaves joined the demonstration. Near Santa Cruz, they encountered an army of police and the uprising was crushed by force. The leaders of the uprising were sentenced to death. To this day, Tula symbolizes the freedom struggle and is extremely important to Curaçaoans.

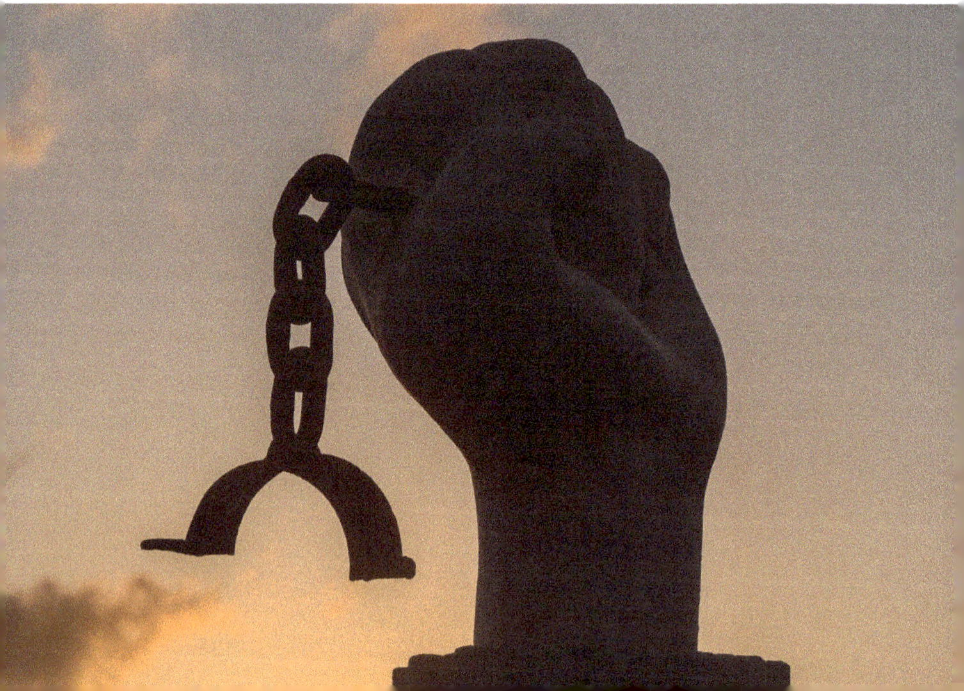

The Tula museum is now housed in the mansion, where an exhibition about the life of slaves on the island and an exhibition of antique furniture can be seen. Besides the Kurá Hulanda museum, the Knip Mansion is well worth a visit to learn about the former life of the slaves on the island. The museum is recently renovated and reopened in februari 2024.

Tula Museum (Landhuis Knip)
Open: Tue - Sun 10am - 4pm | Address: side street of Weg naar Santa Cruz, dir. Playa Kenepa (Knip)
Price: $ 15.- | www.fundashonmuseotula.com | +599 9 687 1771

The Curaçaosch Museum

This museum is located in a former military hospital in Otrobanda. The museum has been home to collections of objects from the 18th , 19th, 20th and 21st century since 1948. The collection consists mainly of furniture, paintings by local and international painters and sculptures. There's also a SNIP cockpit on display, the first KLM aircraft to cross the ocean, from the Netherlands to Curaçao. The museum mainly provides an overview of how people used to live on the island. If you want to learn more on the colonial past of Curaçao we recommend to visit the Kurá Hulanda museum instead.

The Curaçaosch Museum
Open: Tue - Fri 8:30am - 4:30pm, Sat 10am - 4pm
Address: Van Leeuwenhoekstraat, Otrobanda
Price: Adults: NAF 17.50, Children > 5 years NAF 5.75
www.hetcuracaosch.museum | +599 9 462 6051

Maritime Museum

The maritime history of Curaçao goes back more than 500 years. The museum begins with the story of the voyages of discovery from European and Dutch colonization. Maritime history is described based on old nautical maps, ship models, navigation equipment and image and audio. The interior even resembles an old ship deck complete with railings, masts and deck boards. Both early and recent port history is discussed, with the ports of Curaçao serving as a transit port, oil refinery site and cruise ship berth. Finally, the port life of the Dutch Navy, which has a base here, is also discussed extensively. The museum offers various tours, including a tour of the port itself. The Maritime Museum gives a complete and lively picture of the port history of Curaçao.

Maritime Museum
Open: Tue - Thu, Sat 10:30am - 3:30pm
Address: N. Van Den Brandhofstraat 1, Willemstad (Scharloo)
Price: Adults NAF 17.50, Children 6 - 17 years NAF 12.25, Children < 6 years free entrance
www.curacaomaritime.com | +599 9 465 2327

Jewish Culture Historical Museum & Mikvé Israel-Emanuel Synagogue

This museum is part of the Mikvé Israel-Emanuel Synagogue, the oldest synagogue in the Western Hemisphere that has remained in continuous use. The museum is located in the former living area and bath house of the rabbi. There's a patio located in the center of the museum. The museum and the synagogue have been thoroughly restored and many authentic colonial elements have also been restored. 17th- and 18th-century wealth is still evident. The museum houses replicas of engraved tombstones and various ceremonial and cultural objects, such as a Torah (first and most important part of the Jewish Bible), silverware and jewelry.

The synagogue itself contains mahogany furniture, antique brass chandeliers - in which real candles illuminate the synagogue - and the floor is covered with sand, symbolizing the Jewish journey through the desert. A handy bonus in earlier times was that the sand silenced the sound of the services that were being held in secret.

Jewish Culture Historical Museum & Mikvé Israel-Emanuel Synagogue
Open: Mon - Fri 9am - 4:30pm | Services: Fri 6:30pm & Sat 10am (appr. clothing required, free entrance) | Address: Hanchi Snoa 29 (Punda) | Price: NAF 18.- (synagogue & museum)
www.snoa.com | +599 9 461 1067

Kas di Pal'i Maïshi (kunuku house)

Just after slavery was abolished, former slaves built their own shelters in the countryside: the 'cunucu' of Curaçao. The houses were built from the materials that were available at the time: a roof of corn stalks, walls of limestone. Kas di pal'i maïshi therefore means 'house of corn stalks'. Until about 1950 many Curaçaoans lived in this way. Today, only a few of the cunucu houses can be found on the island. The Kas di Pal'i Maïshi Museum is a cunucu cottage restored by the Monument preservation organization, where you can learn more about how Curaçaoans used to live here in the countryside.

Kas di Pal'i Maïshi (kunuku house)
Open: Tue - Sun 10:00am - 2:00pm | Address: Dokterstuin 27 (Weg naar Westpunt)
Price: Adults NAF 10.-, Children NAF 3.50 | +599 9 666 9973

Mansions

After the West India Company could no longer maintain power over the land on the island, plots of land were sold to private individuals. The brand new largescale landowners had impressive mansions built on their land.

Mansion means 'Landhuis' in Dutch. All over Curaçao you can recognise mansions by the word 'Landhuis' in their names.

Architecture

The tropical climate was taken into account in the layout of the houses. Each mansion had at least one spacious veranda, the bedroom was on the cool side and the kitchen on the wind side of the house. No expense was spared to make the house as luxurious as possible. Slaves were purchased and appointed as domestic help, clerks or plantation workers. Smaller houses were built around the mansions where the slaves stayed.

Location

Initially the mansions were mainly built around the central Schottegat, close to the port of Curaçao. Later on, mansions were also built on other parts of the island, between the plantations. The plantation slaves had a terrible existence, in exchange for a minimal salary and 'lodging' they worked the entire days in extremely tough conditions on the plantation fields.

Restoration

Many of the mansions fell into disrepair in the last century, but luckily many of them have also been given a new destination. The architectural delights and chic ornaments have been restored. With the restoration of the mansions, the painful memories of the past also remained alive. We have made a selected list of mansions that are definitely worth visiting.

Restaurants

Many of the other mansions are now operated as catering establishments. *Landhuis Brakkeput Mei Mei* is a good example. Great grill dishes are served out on the spacious terrace. Enjoy your food in the open air under large trees filled with twinkling lights. In addition regular band and salsa nights are organized here. This mansion is located near the Spanish Water on the east side of the island.

Landhuis Dokterstuin is the place to be for good local food. The on-site *Komedor Krioyo* restaurant serves authentic Creole cuisine in the cozy courtyard garden.

Landhuis Chobolobo: Blue Curaçao

The original name of this mansion is 'Zoutpan' ('Salt pan'). The land around Chobolobo was formerly the place where salt was acquired. Because salt was scarce, and therefore costly, it was an important source of income on the downwind islands. At the end of the 18th century the name of the mansion was changed to 'Sebollobo', the meaning of which is still unknown. It is suspected that it's an Indian name.

In 1946, this mansion was known worldwide for its liqueur distillery. In the Second World War liqueurs were very popular as alcoholic beverages, because the beer was of poor quality during that time. Chobolobo is still the distillery for the world famous liqueur Blue Curaçao. On Chobolobo you can take a look in the kitchen at the distillery and, of course, sample this sky blue drink. You can explore Chobolobo on your own or take a guided tour. Finally, enjoy a great lunch, taste the home-made ice cream or drink cocktails in the bar after a tour.

Landhuis Chobolobo
Open: Mon - Fri 8am - 5pm | Tours at 9am/10am/11am/1pm/2pm/3pm
Address: Elias R.A. Moreno Boulevard, Willemstad (Salina) | Price: tours from $ 15.-
www.chobolobo.com | Tel.: +599 9 461 3526

Art

Nena Sanchez

Bright colors, mystical blue women and iconic images of Curaçao are the hallmarks of Nena Sanchez. Nena Sanchez was able to reproduce the colorful Curaçao in her paintings like no other. Her love for the island where she was born and raised is therefore reflected in every artwork she produced. Her paintings can be admired in her gallery and atelier in the Jan Kok mansion and in her gallery in Punda. But you can also view her artworks in the street in the form of murals.

Nena Sanchez - Jan Kok Mansion
Open: Tue - Sat 10am - 5pm | Address: Weg naar Sint Willibrordus
www.nenasanchez.com | +599 9 864 0965

Nena Sanchez - galerie in Punda
Di t/m vr 10am - 5pm | Address: Windstraat 15, Willemstad (wijk Punda)
www.nenasanchez.com | Tel.: +599 9 461 2882

Chichi Curaçao

Chichi sculptures are figurines of Curaçao women who are known as the 'big sis-ters' in their community. A 'big sister' in Curaçao is a caring person that you can always count on. The Chichi figurines were created by Serena Israel, a German artist who emigrated to Curaçao. The big sisters inspired her and the Chichi was born. Because the demand for Chichis grew steadily, she called in the help of local women to manufacture the Chichis with her. More than 50 women paint Chichis for Serena. You can find out which woman made your Chichi via the number on the Chichi you purchased.

Today, Serena Israel manufactures and sells the sculptures in Serena's Art Factory. She also gives workshops, in which you can paint your own Chichi. The Chichis are also for sale at Serena's souvenir store in Punda.

Serena's Art Factory (workshops)
Walk-in workshops: Tue & Sat 9am
Address: Jan Luis 87A (on the road to the Ostrich Farm)
Price: NAF 20.- (excl. costs of the sculpture, from NAF 48.-) | +599 9 738 0648

Chichi Curaçao (store Punda)
Open: Mon - Sat 10am - 5pm | Address: Windstraat, Gomezplein Willemstad (Punda)
www.chichi-curacao.com

Alma Blou Gallery

Alma Blou - 'blue soul' in Papiamento - is a gallery located in Habaai mansion. Habaai mansion is known as one of the most beautiful mansions on Curaçao. It used to be a popular accommodation spot for wealthy families and officers on the island. The gallery exhibits an extensive collection of artwork by local and Caribbean artists. You can buy exclusive souvenirs to your heart's content in the gallery shop. The mansion also has a large sculpture garden where you can relax and enjoy the artwork on show.

Alma Blou Gallery
Open: Tue - Sat 9am - 2pm | Address: Frater Radulphusweg 4
www.galleryalmablou.com | Tel.: +599 9 462 8896

Island- & boat trips

A carefree day out with a guide who will show you the most beautiful places on Curaçao. Or a romantic sunset cruise along the island coast. Book a day trip or excursion and be surprised.

Island trips

For those who are not renting a car or want to enjoy a day out without the car, several island tours are organized on Curaçao. You mostly have the choice of a full or half day on the road, often being picked up and dropped off at your accommodation.

Many of the tours head toward Westpunt and make a stop at one or more beaches. Full-day tours generally include lunch. One well-known tour operator is Irie Tours (www.irietours.com).

Offroad

Literally step off the beaten path and get on a quad or in a jeep. Explore the rugged plains towards Westpunt or be surprised by the flora and fauna in Christoffel Park.

Quads/UTV

Both on the east and west sides of Curaçao, you can book tours where you will discover the more difficult to reach places of Curaçao on a quad or UTV ('utility task vehicle', suitable for several people) accompanied by a guide. Along Curaçao's rugged coasts, there are several plains of volcanic rock. You can't reach these places with an ordinary car. These desolate plains are ideally suited to explore with these off-road vehicles.

Keep in mind that the driver must have a valid driver's license and be at least 21 years old.

Jeepsafari Christoffel Park

You can explore the park by car, as there is a paved road that goes through the park. You can also join a safari tour: a guide will lead you through the highlights of the park with an open jeep and talk about the nature and history of the park and Curaçao. There are tours of two and four hours.

Quads/UTV tours: check www.curacaoactivities.com for different tours.
Jeepsafari Christoffel Park: see www.christoffelpark.org for different tours.

Boat trips

Step aboard a catamaran and enjoy the view from the Caribbean Sea while the captain takes you to the most beautiful snorkeling spots while enjoying a drink. If this is not enjoyment...

Boat trips along the coast of Curaçao

There are several boat trips that sail along the coast of Curaçao. If you like snorkeling, you can choose to go on a snorkeling trip. Sail along the coast for a bit, after which the boat anchors at beautiful snorkeling spots so that everyone can go in the water. Want to go on a romantic tour? Then a 'sunset trip' might be an option for you.

Book a boat trip

On Curaçao there are numerous organisations which offer quite comparable boat trips, all high quality. Some of the most popular organisations are:

Mermaid boat trips: www.mermaidboattrips.com | +599 9 560 1530
Miss Ann boat trips: www.missannboattrips.com | +599 9 560 1367
BlueFinn charters Curaçao: www.bluefinncharters.com | +599 9 690 3717

Powerboat Caribbean

Experience 600HP on the Caribbean Sea. It's now possible to book a boat trip on a rib powerboat and view the coast of Curaçao with a healthy dose of adrenalin. You get to view beautiful places while maneuvering between the waves. A roller coaster pales in comparison. If you're lucky, the dolphins will join you alongside the boat as you race across the sea.

Powerboat Caribbean

Check www.powerboat-caribbean.com for different tours.
+599 9 566 9697 | reservations@powerboat-caribbean.com

Rent a Tiki boat

If you prefer to be the captain yourself, you can rent a Tiki boat on Spanish waters. These are covered round boats, equipped with a round table in the middle and a bench all around. Each tiki boat accommodates six people, including up to four adults.

You don't need a boating license to rent these boats. Each boat has a ladder that allows you to splash into the water while floating around. Optionally, you can rent a tiki boat with barbecue. Meat packages can be included, as well as vegetarian barbecue packages.

Tiki Boats Rental
Open: Mon - Sat 8:30am - 6pm | Rental prices starting from $ 199.- per tiki boat for 1/2 day
Address: Caracasbaaiweg 405-2
www.tikiboatsrental.com | +599 9 682 6644 | info@tikiboatsrental.com

Klein Curaçao

About six miles south of Curaçao is the mere 0.66 square miles, uninhabited island of Klein ('Little') Curaçao. Previously, this island was used to separate the healthy slaves from the sick slaves during the time of the slave trade before they were brought ashore to Curaçao. The sick slaves were quarantined on Klein Curaçao in the designated quarantine building, the remains of which can still be seen.

Today, Klein Curaçao is known as an idyllic paradise bounty island with a limited number of sights including a lighthouse and a shipwreck. Snorkeling off the coast of Klein Curaçao guarantees breathtaking images of the underwater world, with a reasonable chance of spotting a sea turtle.

You can find organizations that offer boat trips to Klein Curaçao everywhere on the island. You can also opt for 'super-fast', with a powerboat, see before mentioned Powerboat Caribbean for more information.

On the southwest coast of the island, various boat trip organizers have built a number of simple accommodations to provide people with daytime comforts such as umbrellas, beach chairs and sanitary facilities. A barbecue lunch is often included.

The passage to Klein Curaçao will take approximately one to two hours, depending on the boat and weather conditions.

Providers of boat trips to Klein Curaçao
Two of the best-known providers are Mermaid Boat Trips (www.mermaidboattrips.com) and Miss Ann Boat Trips (www.missannboattrips.com). The latter even offers the possibility of a true Robinson Crusoe experience: spending the night on the uninhabited island of Klein-Curaçao.

Shopping

Westpunt
Weg naar Westpunt
CHRISTOFFEL PARK
Lagun
Barber
Jan Donker
Soto
Weg naar Santa Cruz
Tera Korá
Jan Kok
Sint Willibrordus
Weg naar Westpunt
Grote Berg
HATO
Jan Kok Baai
Bullenbaai
Weg naar Westp...
Weg naar Bullenbaai
Sint Michiel
Blauwbaai

Shopping

Saliña
Promenade Shopping Center
Bloempot Shopping Center
Zuikertuintje Mall
Santa
Catarina
Brievengat
Bonamweg
Gosieweg
Franklin D. Rooseveltweg
Winston Churchillweg
Ring
Sint Jorisbaai
Ring
Saato Rosaweg
Weg naar Santa Catarina
Santa
Rosa
Seru Loraweg
Weg naar Fuik
WILLEMSTAD
Schottegat
Caracasbanweg
Piscaderabaai
Ring
Saliña
Lagun
Jan Thiel
Spaanse
Water
Oostpunt
Piscadera
Otrobanda
Punda
Pietermaai
Jan Thiel
Santa
Barbara
Caracasbaai
Punda
Mambo Beach Boulevard
Otrobanda
Renaissance Riffort & Kurá Hulanda Village
Sambil Curaçao

Shopping

Spilt a glass of red wine on that beautiful summer dress, or is it time for a new swimsuit? No worries! There are several shopping malls scattered around Curaçao where you'll be able to find everything you need. The following is an overview of the largest shopping malls on the island.

Because Curaçao is the largest transit port in the Caribbean, there are all sorts of things available for sale on the island. This is evident in the diverse range of stores on display. In general, all stores open from eight in the morning to six in the evening: at noon they close for two hours. The catering establishments remain open. Besides Willemstad, there are a number of other shopping malls in the area.

Otrobanda

Since the Renaissance Mall & Rif Fort opened in Otrobanda in 2009, including a luxury shopping street just outside the riffort, Otrobanda has also become interesting for fanatical shoppers. You can go here for, among other things, designer labels and jewelry. In addition, there is also an art gallery where exhibitions are regularly held with works mainly from Curaçao and the Caribbean, but also from other parts of the world.

In the Kurá Hulanda Village you will find several boutiques selling various handmade souvenirs, as well as unique clothing shops and a chocolatier.

Punda

As far back as the 17th century, Punda was already the trading hub of Curaçao. The first streets on the island were built here, right at the entrance to the seaport. The warehouses along the Handelskade show how important this part of the island was for trade. The shopping streets in Punda are perfect for a nice stroll. The range of stores is quite large although the same is often available in those stores. There are various electronics stores that all sell the latest phones, televisions and computer equipment.

Apart from electronics, there is plenty to be had in terms of perfumes and cosmetics. In the famous Penha building, on the corner near the pontoon bridge, a wide range of cosmetic products from well-known brands are on offer and the store windows of the various jewelers are filled with jewelry. The big name clothing brands are also represented.

Finally, there are also plenty of gift stores to be found here and items are also sold on the street. Key rings, towels and inexpensive clothing are distributed through many stores in Punda. For aficionados of cigar smoking, a visit to Cigar Emperium at Gomezplein is a must.

Shopping malls

Sambil

Sambil is a giant, hypermodern shopping mall that is fully covered and AC cooled. Originally, Sambil was a South American concept, with shopping malls in different countries. This complex was opened in Curaçao in 2015, with a wide variety of stores.

While shopping for some new clothing at one of the clothing stores, children can have fun under the supervision of an adult at the indoor playground Kidi's Park. They can also enjoy themselves on the trampolines at Zero Gravity. For the little ones there are several free play corners.

At the central food court you have a wide choice of fast food restaurants. Tired of shopping? Then visit the bowling alley, StrikeZone, or grab a movie in the most advanced cinema on the island: Caribbean Cinema's.

Promenade Shopping Center

With a central location on the island, about 1/2 mile from Saliña, is the Promenade Shopping center on the Schottegatweg-Oost. In this shopping center you can find stylish women's, men's and children's clothing brands. Shoes are imported from countries such as Spain, Italy and the Netherlands and jewelry and watches from Switzerland. In short, you can find everything you need in clothing and accessories right here, all under one roof. For a pit stop, go to Craving Sushi or the lunchroom De Dames.

Bloempot Shopping Center

A thousand feet past the Promenade Shopping center you'll find the Bloempot Shopping center. This shopping center is spacious but the number of stores is limited. You can go here for clothes, shoes and jewelry and there are a few hair salons. Beauty treatments such as manicures and pedicures are also available here. On the large - covered - terrace at Delifrance you can enjoy a refreshing drink and/or lunch.

Zuikertuintje Mall

The adjacent Zuikertuintje Mall was thoroughly renovated a few years ago. It now consists mainly of branches that sell major clothing brands. It also has an optician and a book store. So if you've finished the books you brought with you, just go here for new reading material. Looking for more English books? Visit Mensing's Caminada book store at Schottegatweg-Oost.

Mambo Beach Boulevard

A brand new shopping center is located right by the beach of Mambo Beach. Here you'll find many clothing stores, a tattoo parlor, beauty stores, jewelers and gift stores. All stores are open seven days a week from early till late. Their motto? There's always something to do at Mambo Beach BLVD. In addition to stores, there are also many restaurants and cafés here, ranging from a traditional Dutch snackbar to a sushi restaurant and a Starbucks.

For more information on super markets see page 166.

Snorkeling & diving

Watamula
Westpunt
Weg naar Westpunt
CHRISTOFFEL PARK
Lagun
Barber
Jan Donker
Soto
Weg naar Santa Cruz
Mushroom Forrest
Playa Lagun
Playa Abao
Playa Kalki
Tera Korá
Weg naar Westpunt
Sint Willibrordus
Jan Kok
Grote Berg
Weg naar Westp
Portomari
Jan Kok Baai
Bullenbaai
Weg naar Bullenbaai
Rif St Marie
HATO
Sint Michiel
Blauwbaai
Blue Bay The Wall

Dive sites

Santa
Catarina
Brievengat
Bonamweg
Gosieweg
Weg naar Santa Catarina
Sint Jorisbaai
Franklin D. Rooseveltweg
Winston Churchillweg
Ring
Ring
Ring
Santa Rosaweg
Santa
Rosa
Seru Loraweg
Weg naar Fuik
WILLEMSTAD
Iscaderabaai
Schottegat
Caracasbaaiweg
Piscadera
Otrobanda
Punda
Ring
Saliña
Pietermaai
Lagun
Jan Thiel
Jan Thiel
Spaanse
Water
Oostpunt
East Point
Superior
Producer
Stella Maris
Caracasbaai
Santa
Barbara
Lost Anchor
Tugboat
Smokey's
ORT

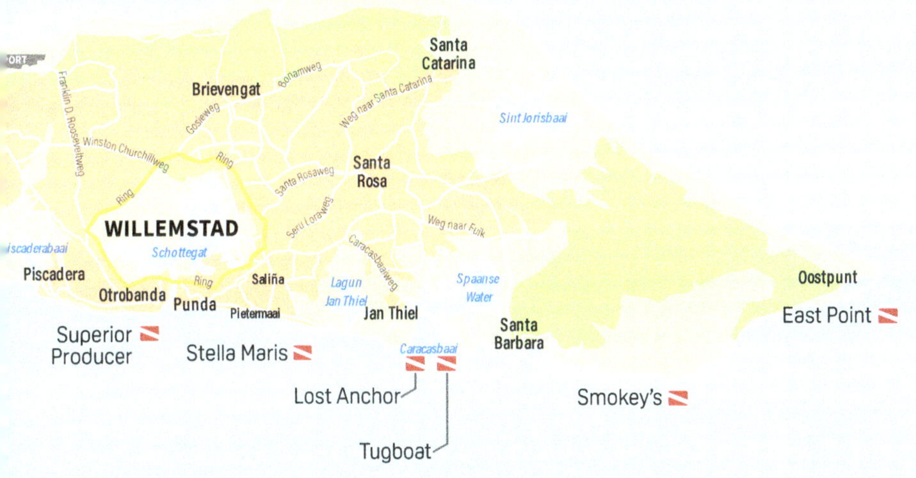

Snorkeling & diving

Curaçao originates from volcanic limestone on which coral has been deposited over many centuries. Off the coast of Curaçao are beautiful coral reefs, home to an array of flora and fauna. Brightly colored tropical fish, seahorses, sea turtles and barracudas are among the many inhabitants of the underwater world that surrounds Curaçao. If you don't like diving, then a snorkeling set is also enough to enjoy the under water splendor.

Snorkeling

If you go on vacation to Curaçao then a snorkeling set is one of the most important travel items you can have. There are several beaches where you can enjoy the beautiful tropical fish that live in the Caribbean Sea just feet from the coast. In addition, various snorkeling trips are organized to take you to well-known spots around the island.

Purchasing a snorkeling set: what to pay attention to

You can purchase a snorkeling set for a few bucks in one of the many diving stores on Curaçao. When fitting the mask (goggles) it is important that the mask closes properly and is sealed around the edges. You can easily test this by pushing the mask against your face without putting the strap around your head and then breathing in through your nose. If the mask fits properly, it should stay on your face without you holding it.

Snorkeling beaches

You can take out your snorkeling set on almost all the beaches that you come across from Willemstad towards Westpunt. There's always something to see underwater, anywhere around the island. For an overview of all beaches, see page 40 and further. We've highlighted a few beaches here that are ideal for snorkeling.

PortoMari

At PortoMari there are several reef balls in the water just a few feet from the coast. These concrete balls are teeming with tropical fish that you can observe closely with a snorkel.

Playa Lagun & Playa Abao

At Playa Lagun and Playa Abao (Grote Knip), you can see beautiful fish along the rocks. If you swim a bit, you come to the drop-off, where the seabed slopes abruptly and the coral reef begins. It is really enjoyable here in clear waters and sunny weather! Beware, however, for boats and water scooters that, particularly in the weekends, often sail across the bay towards the beach.

Playa Kalki

On the beach of Playa Kalki, which has been nicknamed *Alice in Wonderland*, there are always divers present. There's also a diving store here. In addition to stunningly colorful fish, the mushroom-shaped coral formations are something to look forward to.

Playa grandi (playa piskado)

Located near Westpunt, this traditionally serene fisherman's beach has experienced a surge in popularity in recent years, thanks in large part to the presence of sea turtles gracefully gliding around the pier. Put on your mask and immerse yourself in an encounter with these magnificent creatures, but don't touch them.

Snorkeling trips

There are many snorkeling trips on Curaçao, both at diving schools and on cruises around the island. Often you'll end up at the same snorkeling sites, so it's a smart idea to compare prices.

Tugboat

Many of these snorkeling trips lead to the familiar tugboat, undoubtedly the most beautiful snorkeling spot on the island. This tugboat that sank more than 30 years ago is only a few feet under water. The boat has been swallowed up by coral and plants that, in recent decades, formed a shelter for many tropical fish species. The boat and the fish around it provide fantastic photo opportunities, which would not be out of place on a postcard. Be careful, however, that you do not touch the boat, it is partly rusted and also covered with different types of coral that can cause irritation.

There's also plenty to see in the rock formations next to the tugboat. In the caverns in the rocks, you can often see moray eels, scorpion fish and crabs. You should not be surprised if you suddenly find yourself fishing between an entire school, that often swim with the current along the rock faces. You can also come here by car, see page 156.

Aquafari

One of the most unique attractions on Curaçao is Aquafari. On a futuristic-looking underwater scooter, you float among the fish under the supervision of a professional diver. Ideal if you're unable to, or don't want to, go diving, but still want to explore the world underwater. For more information see Aquafari.net or visit Aquafari in Piscadera, next to Pirate Bay.

Aquafari
Tours: daily at 10am, 12am and 2pm
Address: Canoaweg 11, Boca Sami | Price: from $ 139.- per person
www.aquafari.net | +5 99 9 513 2526

Diving

For real underwater enthusiasts there is only one option, of course, and that's with a tank on your back descending along the spectacular coral reefs that are scattered around Curaçao. Also, or perhaps correctly, for those who have never been diving before, this is an excellent opportunity to get acquainted with the sport. The courses that are offered in Curaçao are generally of high quality and PADI certified. It is very pleasant to learn to dive in Curaçao in the warm water surrounded by tropical fish.

Introductory dive

A common phrase is: "diving is not for me". If you fall into that category, then it is really worth considering an introductory diving session, without obligation. This can be done for very little money at most recognized diving schools on the island. You don't descend far during the test dive, it is mainly about getting used to the equipment and moving around underwater. This way you can familiarize yourself with the sport and get a taste of the fascinating underwater world. Inquire at one of the many diving schools about the options available to you; who knows, you might just love it.

Diving courses

Diving courses are available at all levels, for beginners and advanced. During a beginners course, also called PADI open water course, the most important thing is to familiarize yourself with the diving equipment and to practice a lot of possible emergency situations under water. These exercises are of course done in a very controlled way and you learn what to do in the sea in certain situations.

You'll learn this partly in practice during the various dives you will go on with a small class of divers, but a large part of it is theory. Before you can complete the course you must first take an exam. All in all, the course lasts about three days. Once you've successfully completed them - and practice shows that the success rate is pretty much 100% - you are authorized to hire diving equipment all over the world and start diving. The only limitation is that you may 'only' dive to a depth of 60 feet.

You can also follow advanced courses. Here you dive to a depth of about 100 feet and there are opportunities to go boat diving, diving for wreckages and/or night diving. This is not only about the art of diving, but also about diving more adventurously and more actively.

Buddy

In diving, there is one restriction that always applies: you are never allowed to go diving on your own. From the basic course you will learn to dive with a buddy. A buddy is your underwater partner, and you should always keep an eye on each other. During the course you will also learn how to communicate with your buddy under water, and how you can help each other in an emergency situation. Are you the only diver in your travel group? Then contact one of the diving schools on the island, often they form buddy teams during boat trips or a supervised dive.

The most beautiful diving locations

If you have your diving license, then nothing stands in the way of jumping into the deep. Every diving school on Curaçao has a varied range of guided dives, but also possibilities to rent equipment and to dive independently (with buddy).

On the following pages you will find a selection of diving locations around the island that are recommended by experienced divers as the most beautiful locations.

West of Willemstad

Wata Mula

This is the northernmost diving spot on Curaçao, with a rugged and authentic underwater world. The flora and fauna at Wata Mula are truly spectacular and unique. There is also an underwater cave. There are large walls at the bottom and occasionally sharks and turtles can be seen here.

Playa Kalki

Playa Kalki is located near Westpunt and is the perfect place for sun lovers, divers and snorkelers. Kalki means limestone in Papiamento and refers to the limestone in the cliffs. In general, the waves are calm and the current is weak. The beach consists of sand and is covered with different types of hard coral. There are morays, crabs, mushroom-shaped coral formations and multicolored reef fish. When you reach 100 feet or deeper you discover large areas where table and leaf coral live.

Mushroom Forest

Mushroom Forest owes its name to the enormous forest of mushroom-shaped coral formations. Many fish and other sea animals find shelter between these giant formations. Mushroom Forest is therefore a unique diving spot. It's best to go to Mushroom Forest by boat, because it is quite far from the beach of Playa Lagun. In addition, the existing cliffs don't make it easy to access Mushroom Forest. You can book a boat trip to this amazing diving spot, through various different diving schools.

PortoMari

PortoMari is also a beautiful and unique diving spot on Curaçao because of the many fish and the double reef, which is easily accessible here. It's also because of the double reef and the valley in between that it's known as The Valley. PortoMari has a flat sandy bottom and you can see rare fish such as pairs of cornet fish and sometimes small nurse sharks and eagle rays. Other reef fish that you can see include squid, angel and parrotfish, groupers, yellowtail snappers, trumpet fish and stingrays.

Superior Producer

The Superior Producer is an overgrown wreckage that lies at a depth of more than 100 feet, just outside the entrance of St. Anna Bay. In 1977 the ship sailed out of the harbor, on the way to Isla Margarita, when it let in water. The ship was unfortunately no longer salvageable. It was then dragged out of the harbor and allowed to sink. After all these years the ship has been completely swallowed up by coral, and you can see several reef fish, barracudas, groupers, corals and anemones here.

From Willemstad you follow the road along the coast in a westerly direction and parallel to the Aqualectra factory, follow the signs for Double reef. A supervised dive is recommended, because it is quite difficult to determine the exact position of the ship and the current can be treacherous.

East of Willemstad

East Point

East Point or Oostpunt is, as the name suggests, located on the easternmost point of the island. This diving spot can only be reached by boat. There is a naturally formed underwater bridge of coral. Sharks, barracudas, eagle rays and sea turtles can regularly be spotted here.

Lost Anchor

This diving site is characterized by a particularly bright and colorful environment and a lushly vegetated drop-off. On the seabed there is an anchor that is now completely overgrown with coral, hence the name of this site. There are also many seahorses to see here.

Smokey´s

After a boat trip of about 20 minutes from Mambo Beach Boulevard, you'll arrive at this unique diving spot. The underwater world here is characterized by clear water that offers perfect views. Sharks and stingrays are regularly seen at this spot.

Restaurants

Westpunt
1
Weg naar Westpunt
CHRISTOFFEL PARK
Lagun
Jan Donker
Barber
Soto
Weg naar Santa Cruz
Tera Korá
2
Sint Willibrordus
Jan Kok
Grote Berg
Jan Kok Baai
Weg naar Westpunt
3
Bullenbaai
Weg naar Bullenbaai
Sint Michiel
Blauwbaai
4
ST. ANNABAAI
5
BREEDESTRAAT
WESTSTRAAT
BOLDINGSTRAAT
SCHARLOOWEG
VAN DE BRANDHOFSTRAAT
Scharloo
SCHARLOOWEG
GOSIEWEG
SCHARLOOWEG
PLASA MUNDO MERCED
PATER EUWENSWEG
Renaissance Mall & Rif Fort
Renaissance Mall & Rif Fort
waaigat
HANDELSKADE
SHA CAPRILES
CONCORDIASTRAAT
BREEDESTRAAT
DE RUYTERKADE
A. DE VEERSTRAAT
Otrobanda
6
PLASA PIAR
FORTPLEIN
PRINSENSTRAAT
NIEUWESTRAAT
7
10
ANSINGHSTRAAT
JULIANAPLEIN
BERG ALTENA
WATERFORTSTRAAT
HENDRIK PLEIN
PIETERMAAI
8 9
JUN GODETT
PENSTRAAT
ORANJESTRAAT
Punda
Pietermaai
11

Restaurants

1. Jaanchies
2. Landhuis Daniël
3. Karakter
4. Brass Boer
5. Gouverneur de Rouville
6. Plein Café Wilhelmina
7. Mundo Bizarro
8. BijBlauw
9. De Heeren at Sea
10. Kome
11. Mosa/Caña
12. Poké Food Station
13. Nultwintig
14. Baoase Beach Restaurant
15. Sea Side Terrace
16. Chill Beach Bar & Grill
17. Landhuis Brakkeput Mei Mei
18. Omundo

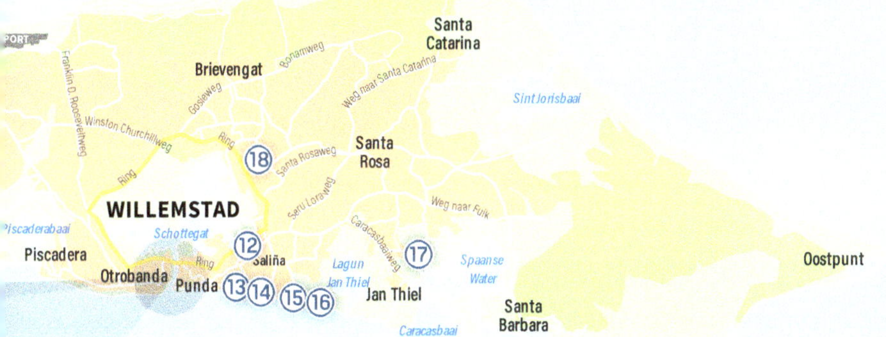

Restaurants

Because Curaçao is relatively close to the equator, the sun goes down pretty early. On average, it gets dark at seven o'clock in the evening in Curaçao. What could be better than to enjoy a refreshing drink at the end of the afternoon and see the sun set during a romantic dinner. In this chapter you'll find an independent selection of the many restaurants that Curaçao has to offer.

Restaurants on Curaçao

Curaçao has more than 300 restaurants, which are spread over the island. Most are located in or near Willemstad and at the popular beaches east of Willemstad. The price level doesn't differ that much from major cities in the USA and western Europe; a main course costs around USD 20.

In general, the restaurants on Curaçao are rated very highly. The fierce competition on the island means they have to deliver quality. At most restaurants, the nine-percent sales tax is included in the price. Some restaurants also include the tip in the price, which is specified in the menu.

Traditional cuisine

The original Curaçaon cuisine is unique in the world. Just like the population, the Curaçao kitchen originated from many different cultures and influences. Unique to Curaçao are the pastchi (patties) and stoba (stewed meat). Many dishes are also served with pica, a spicy pepper sauce. Since Curaçao is an island, meals often include fish in some form or other.

Places where you can still enjoy the traditional Antillean food include the old market hall in Willemstad (Plasa Bieu), Jaanchies Restaurant, Restaurant Rozendaels and Seaside Terrace.

International cuisine

Because Curaçao attracts many international visitors, it's not surprising that a lot of restaurants serve mainly international dishes. Most have a varied menu, with a choice of fish, meat and vegetarian dishes. Incidentally, there are also several specialty restaurants that revolve more around Japanese (sushi) or Indonesian dishes, for example.

Our selection of restaurants

We've made an independent selection of 18 restaurants from the many restaurants on Curaçao. This selection is based on several factors. The price/quality ratio and the distinctive character of a restaurant are most important.

The quality score is based on the average of hundreds of reviews. The average price level is determined on the basis of the average price of a main course, starting with < $ 15.- and raising in steps of $ 5.- to > $ 30.-.

Current information: scan the QR codes

Opening hours may change from time to time. Therefore, scan a restaurant's QR code to find the most up-to-date information (internet connection required). You can also view the menu and find theme nights on many websites. Increasingly, you can also book a table online.

Jaanchies

★★★☆☆ | $$$$$

Jaanchies is a known concept in Curaçao, partly because of the impressive owner (the 'speaking menu'), the whistling sugar snatchers and the decor from grandmother's time. Go here if you've always wanted to eat iguana, or just to have a drink.

🍴 Local cuisine
🕐 Daily 12pm - 6pm
📞 +599 9 864 0126
📍 Weg naar Westpunt z/n

Landhuis Daniël

★★★★☆ | $$$$$

Whether you come by for a cup of coffee with a tasty snack or go for lunch or dinner, at this 18th century mansion you're in the right place. The menu is diverse and offers something for everyone, from pizza to a rice table.

🍴 International & eastern cuisine
🕐 Mon 12pm - 2pm & 5pm - 10pm
  Tue - Sat 8am - 2pm & 5pm - 10pm
  Sun 8am - 10pm
📞 +599 9 864 8400
📍 Weg naar Westpunt z/n

Karakter

☆☆☆☆☆ | $$$$

Away from the crowds, right at sea, is the terrace that belongs to Karakter. If you eat here, you can use the beach chairs for free during the day. You need your ID when you enter the resort.

🍽 International cuisine
🕐 Daily 8am - 9pm
📞 +599 9 864 2233
📍 Coral Estate Resort, St. Willibrordus

Brass Boer

☆☆☆☆☆ | $$$$$

If you want to enjoy an evening of haute cuisine in the form of creative and surprising dishes, this is the place to be. This restaurant by renowned star chef Johnny Boer, known for the famous dutch 3-star restaurant *De Librije*, is located on the corner of Blue Bay beach. Book early if you want to dine here.

🍽 International cuisine
🕐 Daily 12pm - 10pm
   On Tuesday closed for dinner
📞 +599 9 869 7215
📍 Blue Bay resort

Gouverneur de Rouville

★★★★☆ | $$$$○

Admire the ships entering Willemstad from a table on the balcony or find a spot in the beautiful backyard. End your evening in the cocktail bar next door. It's a good idea to reserve ahead if you want to dine on the balcony.

🍴 International cuisine
🕐 Daily 9am - 12pm
📞 +599 9 462 5999
📍 De Rouvilleweg 9-F, Otrobanda

Plein Café Wilhelmina

★★★★☆ | $$○○○

Fancy a simple but tasty bite or a refreshing drink? You can! In the heart of Punda all day on the cozy terrace of this typical dutch eatery. They also offer a cheap daily menu (first come first served!).

🍴 International cuisine
🕐 Daily 7am - 10pm
📞 +599 9 461 9666
📍 Wilhelminaplein 19-23, Punda

BijBlauw

☆☆☆☆☆ | $$$$

In a courtyard between the monumental buildings of the Pietermaai district in Willemstad you can enjoy a farm-fresh breakfast or a high-quality lunch or dinner directly by the sea. If you want to dine right by the sea, reserve a table in advance.

🍴 International cuisine
🕐 Daily 8am - 10pm
📞 +599 9 650 0551
📍 Pietermaai 82-84

De Heeren at Sea

☆☆☆☆ | $$$

Enjoy the sunset, with your feet in the sand, the sound of the sea in combination with a snack and a drink. Experience the true Caribbean atmosphere and hospitality. Try the famous Breakfast Basket or the extensive bbq evening.

🍴 International cuisine
🕐 Daily 8am - 12pm
📞 +599 9 465 2575
📍 Pietermaai 104

Kome

☆☆☆☆⯪ | ⑤⑤⑤⑤⑤

In the Pietermaai district you can find the Kome restaurant. The strength of this restaurant is the creative chef who has put together an original menu, where the meat is prepared on a wood grill. The popular tapas evening takes place on Wednesdays. Reservations recommended.

🍴 Caribbean cuisine

🕐 Tue - Sat 12pm - 10pm
Brunch: Sat 11am - 3pm

📞 +599 9 465 0413

📍 Joh. van Walbeeckplein 6, Pietermaai

Mundo Bizarro

☆☆☆☆☆ | ⑤⑤⑤⑤⑤

If you didn't know better you'd swear that you've arrived in Cuba. The colorful and cozy interior makes Mundo Bizarro a unique restaurant experience, especially if you're here during one of the weekly live music sessions on Saturday.

🍴 International & Local cuisine

🕐 Daily 8am - 1pm

📞 +599 9 461 6767

📍 Nieuwestraat 12, Punda

Mosa/Caña

☆☆☆☆☆ | $$$$$

At Mosa/Caña, creativity and quality go hand in hand. The monthly changing menu consists of both regular and smaller dishes you can share. You can admire murals by local artists around the terrace.

🍴 Latin/Caribbean fusion cuisine

🕐 Tue - Sat 18am - 12pm

📞 +599 9 691 5429
(reservations through Whatsapp)

📍 Penstraat 41

Restaurant Nultwintig

☆☆☆☆☆ | $$$$$

Opened in 2019, this stylish restaurant was created by top Dutch chefs. The name is a reference to Amsterdam's conviviality. From the terrace you look out over the sea while enjoying the excellent special dishes. End your evening at the cocktail bar.

🍴 International cuisine

🕐 Mon - Sat 12pm - 12pm
Sun 10am - 12pm

📞 +599 9 465 6066

📍 Penstraat 300

Baoase Beach Restaurant

☆☆☆☆☆ | ⑤⑤⑤⑤⑤

One of the island's best restaurants, with chef René Klop (La Rive, Amstel Hotel Amsterdam) at the helm. At the Beach Restaurant, you can dine à la carte or choose a 4-course or 5-course menu. At the adjacent Sunset Deck Restaurant, there is a changing theme from Wednesday through Sunday, from Asian to BBQ.

🍽 International & Asian cuisine
🕐 Daily 7am - 10pm
📞 +599 9 461 1799
📍 Winterswijkstraat 2

Sea Side Terrace

☆☆☆☆☆ | ⑤⑤⑤⑤⑤

A sea container that has been converted into a kitchen, a few plastic chairs and some lights. And delicious fresh fish in combination with an extremely relaxed atmosphere. Experience the Antillean hospitality on a small bay just outside Willemstad.

🍽 Local cuisine
🕐 Tue - Sun 12pm - 10pm
📞 +599 9 461 8361
📍 Dr Martin Luther King Blvd

Chill Beach Bar and Grill

☆☆☆☆☆ | $$$

After a day of sunbathing on Mambo Beach, there's nothing better than falling into one of the chill hammocks with an ice cold beer or a nice cocktail. Hungry? Enjoy the famous fish and meat skewers at one of the picnic tables.

🍴 International cuisine

🕐 Daily 9am - 10pm

📞 +599 9 434 8888

📍 Mambo Beach Boulevard

Omundo

☆☆☆☆☆ | $$$

Stylish yet cozy, with no less than 20 wines that can be ordered by the glass. The menu consists of dishes from all over the world, from Beef Wellington to a Mexican taco to Curaçao's pride: 'Truki Pan'. Once a month, you can have all-you-can-eat sushi or enjoy an Indonesian buffet.

🍴 Interational & Local cuisine

🕐 Mon - Sat 12pm - 10pm

📞 +599 9 738 8477

📍 Suikertuintjeweg

Landhuis Brakkeput Mei Mei

☆☆☆☆☆ | ⑤⑤⑤⑤⑤

On the attractive terrace of the historic mansion, you can eat dishes prepared on the traditional charcoal grill. The menu also features a variety of other appetizers and cocktails. Wednesday through Sunday, children can visit the miniature golf course and tropical playground from 4pm.

🍴 Caribbean cuisine & grill

🕐 Daily 5pm - 11pm

📞 +599 9 767 1500

📍 Kaminda Brudernan Tue Brakkapoti

Poké Food Station

☆☆☆☆☆ | ⑤⑤⑤⑤⑤

No idyllic seaside location and 5-course chef's menu. But the friendly staff and delicious fresh ingredients make up for all that. Create your own pokébowl and enter your choices on the order form. Your pokébowl is made on the spot. You can eat it here or take it with you.

🍴 Asian cuisine

🕐 Daily 11am - 10pm

📞 +599 9 461 4441

📍 Fokkerweg 28, Saliña

Chill
&
Grill
LowBudget Autoverhuur →10 km
tel. 523-3483/512-5363
PAERDESTAL

Nightlife & events

Westpunt
Weg naar Westpunt
CHRISTOFFEL PARK
Lagun
Jan Donker
Barber
Soto
Weg naar Santa Cruz
Tera Korá
Weg naar Westpunt
Jan Kok
Sint Willibrordus
Grote Berg
HATO
Weg naar Westpunt
Jan Kok Baai
Bullenbaai
Weg naar Bullenbaai
Sint Michiel
Blauwbaai
Kokomo Beach

Nightlife

Pirate Bay
Caribbean Cinemas
Santa Catarina
Brievengat
Bonamweg
Weg naar Santa Catarina
Sint Jorisbaai
Franklin D. Roseveltweg
Gosieweg
Winston Churchillweg
Ring
Santa Rosaweg
Santa Rosa
Ring
WILLEMSTAD
Schottegat
Seru Loraweg
Weg naar Fuik
Piscaderabaai
Caracasbaaiweg
Ring
Saliña
Lagun Jan Thiel
Spaanse Water
Oostpunt
Piscadera
Otrobanda
Punda
Jan Thiel
Caracasbaai
Santa Barbara
Netto Bar
Zanzibar
The Movies Otrobanda
Mambo Beach Boulevard
Saint Tropez Ocean Club
Mundo Bizarro
The Movies Punda

Nightlife & events

When the sun sets at 7 o'clock in the evening, the Curaçaoans sound in the nightlife. This has been happening for years during the famous happy hours. Every day of the week there is a beach bar that keeps happy hour by night. The drinks are then half the price, for an hour, the music goes a tad louder and the feet start to move on the dancefloor. Even after the happy hours the night has plenty to offer: go salsa dancing at a salsa workshop, drink cocktails in Pietermaai or dance the night away in one of Curaçao's nightclubs.

Happy hours

Happy hours are popular on Curaçao. This isn't only due to the favorable prices, but also because happy hours guarantee a pleasant crowd. The volume goes to level ten or a band or DJ will play live. At some beach spots there are snacks around or the barbecue is getting started.

In this chapter you'll find some of the most popular happy hours, sorted by day. For a complete overview, check out the free magazine available everywhere on the island: *Esaki Tin*, or online esaki-tin.com.

Friday
Mambo Beach Boulevard
The beach at Mambo Beach Boulevard is home to several beach bars that hold happy hours at various times on Wednesdays, Fridays and Sundays. If you want to kick off the weekend festively, this beach is the place to be.

Start the evening at Chill Beach Bar, with happy hour starting at 5pm. A laid back beach bar where you can also have great food at the picnic tables on the beach. At 5:30pm, Bonita and Hemingway also kick off with their happy hours. At the latter, you can also enjoy live music from 8pm. Time to move your feet!

At Wet & Wild, the party also gets going from 8pm, with happy hour until 9pm. If you really want to go all out, then the happy hour at the Madero Ocean Club is highly recommended, starting at 10pm. You can dance and have drinks here into the night.

Mambo Beach Boulevard
Address: Bapor Kibra | www.mambobeach.com

Saturday

Zanzibar

Every Saturday from 5pm to 6pm is happy hour at Zanzibar. This happy hour is one of the busiest on the island. Live bands or DJs often play, and snacks from the barbecue are available.

In addition to the regular happy hours, there are also often events, parties and concerts. Every Wednesday night is dedicated to unplugged beach sessions: acoustic music in a romantic setting. Zanzibar is located in Jan Thiel Bay. Both Zanzibar and one of the adjacent restaurants are open for dinner, so you can conveniently sit down here right after drinks.

Zanzibar
Address: Jan Thielbaai | www.janthielbeach.com

Sunday

Kokomo Beach

On Sunday evenings from 5pm to 6pm, it is happy hour at Kokomo Beach with live music. Kokomo Beach is located west of Willemstad, halfway down the Weg naar Bullenbaai. It is a household name on the island, not only as a beach, but also as an entertainment venue. In addition, you can dine there from Tuesday to Saturday between 6pm and 9:30pm. Every month there is the famous full moon party. See the website for the events calendar.

Kokomo Beach
Address: Vaersenbaai | www.kokomo-beach.com
The full moon party requires tickets, which can be bought online.

Mambo Beach Boulevard

Did you kick off the weekend on Friday during the many happy hours at Mambo Beach and are you eager for more? Then end your weekend on Sunday evening here as well. Happy hours are almost identical to those on Fridays.

Daily

Saint Tropez Ocean Club

Enjoy the happy hour from 6pm to 7pm every day while the sun sets on the outskirts of Willemstad. Moreover, every Monday is dedicated to sushi and cocktails, with special prices for cocktails.

In addition, Saint Tropez has an extensive, international menu that covers everything from breakfast to dinner. The club is located by the water in Pietermaai and has a beautiful sea view. In the middle of the club is an infinity pool where you feel like you're in the French Riviera by day. Around the pool are lounge chairs and cabanas to dream away on while the sun sets on the outskirts of Willemstad.

Saint Tropez Ocean Club
Address: Pietermaai 152 | www.sainttropezcuracao.com

Mundo Bizarro

Every day between 5:30pm and 6:30pm, this Cuban café/restaurant has happy hour, with live music on Saturdays. Mundo Bizarro is located in Pietermaai, and besides tasty drinks, it also has a great kitchen. So afterwards, a delicious dinner is a good option. See also page 118.

Mundo Bizarro
Address: Nieuwstraat 12 (Pietermaai) | www.mundobizarrocuracao.com

Pirate Bay

Every day, this beach club, located in the Piscadera bay to the west of Willemstad, has a happy hour from 5pm to 6pm. On Fridays there's an extra long happy hour, from 4pm to 6pm with live music. Pirate Bay is also a restaurant with an extensive menu, where you can have dinner on the beach. It's recommended to make a reservation if you want to have dinner here.

As the name suggests, it's like you've arrived on the set of the Pirates of the Caribbean. The grinning pirate dolls complete the picture with the dark interior and the metal chandeliers. Pirate Bay also organizes other events in addition to the happy hours and it's a popular wedding location.

Pirate Bay
Address: Piscadera Bay | www.piscaderabeach.com

Netto Bar

You don't visit this pub for a happy hour, but more importantly for the fact that it's the oldest bar on the island. The bar was founded by the late Ernesto 'Netto' Koster, an icon in Willemstad. Net's biggest dream was to run a bar in his own neighborhood. In 1954 he made his dream come true and he worked in the Netto Bar until he was 87 years old. The bar is worth a visit for the interior alone. The bar is full of pictures and paintings of the idyllic Curaçao and of Netto with famous guests in his bar, like the Dutch King Willem Alexander.

On Friday night there is often live music and the feet get moving on the dancefloor. While enjoying the bright green, homemade drinks known as *Róm Bèrdè*, you can dance the night away.

In case you still want to know… the weekly happy hour is on Monday at 6pm.

Netto Bar
Adres: Breedestraat 143 (Otrobanda) | www.facebook.com/nettobar

Annual events

New year's eve

There are a lot of fireworks on show on the island in the days leading up to new year's eve. In particular, the *pagaras*, deafening 100,000 firecrackers, can be heard and felt everywhere. Various large fireworks shows are organized in and around Willemstad.

From time to time there are beach concerts by popular, mostly Dutch, artists and DJs. Keep an eye on the announcements on the island to see where you need to be and make sure to buy your concert tickets in time.

Fuikdag

On the first Sunday of the new year, when the champagne and new year's eve snacks are still being digested, Curaçaon partygoers head to Fuikbaai. This bay transforms into an unorganized chaos of boats and party people. In recent years there have been several top DJs such as Afrojack and Martin Garrix who put on a surprise live performance, from their own boat or from the floating stage. You can only come here by boat. So you can rent a boat yourself, but there are also boat owners who sell spots on their private boats.

King's day (April 27th)

The population of Curaçao is very much a fan of royalty, evident from the many state portraits you encounter in government buildings, among other things. As such, King's Day doesn't pass by quietly on Curaçao. All of Willemstad turns orange on King's Day, with lots of market stalls and bands filling the streets. Top Dutch artists regularly give concerts on King's Day or the night before. Especially in Pietermaai, King's night is celebrated exuberantly.

Carnival

Compared to other carnival celebrations in the world, carnival on Curaçao is characterized by the fusion of all different cultures. Each culture shaped the current carnival on Curaçao with its own rituals. During the carnival period that takes place annually from January to the beginning of March, all kinds of parades, parties, competitions and other events are organized. Everywhere you look you can eat, drink and enjoy the music and the joy being had everywhere. The entire island is under the spell of this event of the people.

Parades

The carnival period ends with two large parades, the 'Gran Marcha' ('big parade') and the 'Farewell Parade'. The Gran Marcha is held on the Sunday before Ash Wednesday, the Farewell Parade takes place on the Tuesday before Ash Wednesday. For the next years you can find the exact dates below:

	2025	2026	2027
Gran Marcha	March 2nd	February 15th	February 7th
Farewell Parade	March 4th	February 17th	February 9th

Seú parade

Every year on Easter Monday the 'Seú parade' takes place, also called the 'Harvest Festival Parade' or the 'Harvest Festival'. Until the beginning of the 20th century this procession passed over the agricultural fields. Unique to this parade is the 'Wapa' dance, which imitates movements of sowing and harvesting. Due to the arrival of the oil refinery and the decrease of agriculture, the procession now passes through the center of Willemstad.

Curaçao North Sea Jazz Festival

Almost every year (since 2010) at the end of August / beginning of September, Curaçao organizes a special edition of the North Sea Jazz festival with world-class artists. In the past this has included names such as Tom Jones, Lenny Kravitz, Lionel Richie, John Legend, Sting and Jason Derulo. It is recommended to book your tickets early.

Curaçao North Sea Jazz Festival
Location: World Trade Center Curaçao | www.curacaonorthseajazz.com

Cinemas

Curaçao has three large cinemas where you can watch all of the latest international movie hits. These cinemas are all located in or next to Willemstad.

The Movies Punda

The Movies is the oldest cinema in Curaçao, but it's still modern. Although the building looks traditional, the rooms are equipped with the latest visual and audio technology. They also show 3D-movies here.

The Movies Punda
Address: Plaza Mundo Merced (Scharloo)
Movie schedule: themoviescuracao.com/punda

The Movies Otrobanda

This cinema opened its doors under the name The Cinemas in 2009, as part of the large Renaissance hotel in Otrobanda. The name was later changed to the same name as the cinema that was already located in Punda: The Movies. So the cinema in Otrobanda is the newest of The Movies' two locations. The programming of both cinemas is fairly coordinated with little overlap, making the total selection of cinema movies on Curaçao quite large.

The cinema is equipped with no less than six different theaters, all equipped with digital screens and perfect sound. Two theaters even show exclusively 3D films. The movie theater has an American feel, mainly because of the huge servings of popcorn and Coke and the complete fast food menus available.

The Movies Otrobanda
Address: Baden Powellweg 1 (Renaissance Riffort)
Movie schedule: themoviescuracao.com/otrobanda

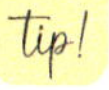

To the movies at a discount

On Mondays through Wednesdays, go to The Movies at a discount. You then pay only NAF 8 for a 2D film. 3D films are also attractively priced on these days.

Caribbean Cinemas

Caribbean Cinemas is the newest cinema in Curaçao and is located in Sambil, the huge shopping mall, just a ten-minute drive west of Willemstad. This is the cinema of all cinemas, with comfortable leather seats, perfect picture and sound quality and, last but not least, so-called D-box chairs. These chairs move in sync with the movie, for an even more intense experience.

Caribbean cinemas
Address: Veeris 27 (Sambil) | Movie schedule: www.caribbeancinemas.com/curacao

Warm clothes

Don't forget to put on long pants or other warm clothes before you go to the movies, the cinema halls can be quite chilly with the air conditioning.

Routes

The wild
west

3 Shete Boka Park
2 Christoffel Park
1 Hòfi Pastor
Westpunt
CHRISTOFFEL PARK
Lagun
Jan Donker
Barber
Soto
Weg naar Santa Cruz
Tera Korá
Sint Willibrordus
Jan Kok
Grote Berg
Jan Kok Baai
Bullenbaai
Weg naar Bullenbaai
Sint Michiel
Blauwbaai
4 Landhuis Knip
5 Playa Abao
Restaurant Playa Forti
Playa Forti
Playa Westpunt

Route 1

Open this route in
Google Maps

The 'wild west' of Curaçao

As soon as you drive 15 minutes west of Willemstad, there isn't much left of the picturesque city center, the tourist attractions or the beautiful little restaurants. The west side of the island - apart from the occasional small sleepy village - is unspoilt and remote. Nature is in charge here and determines the surroundings. Of course there is plenty of fun to be had along the coast on the dozens of beaches but, if you follow this route, you'll discover that the outback also has its charm and a lot of beauty to offer.

Although the distances on Curaçao are relatively small, a single journey to Westpoint takes just under an hour. The roads are not all of equal quality yet and motorways don't exist in Curaçao. On average, people drive 50 mph (80 km/h) on the main roads.

About this route

We start the route in Willemstad. At the top of each page you can find the directions, with an indication of the duration of the route. This route takes a full day, but can be cut short, if desired, by skipping certain parts.

Using Google Maps offline

If you have a Wi-Fi connection, you can download the map of Curaçao on Google Maps. Scan the QR code on the previous page while on Wi-Fi and this route will automatically open in Google Maps. If you turn on GPS along the way, you can navigate the island without an internet connection for free.

Willemstad → Hòfi Pastor

From Otrobanda, exit the roundabout at the bus station on Pater Eeuwensweg.

Go straight at the first roundabout and the upcoming intersections with traffic lights. At the big roundabout follow the signs to Westpunt. Pay attention to the priority rules at this roundabout!

After about 30 minutes you will reach the village of Barber where you'll find the entrance to Hòfi Pastor next to the church.

Hòfi Pastor

Hòfi Pastor is a hiking/walking area with a fairytale atmosphere. The area owes its fame mainly to the ancient and gigantic *Kapok tree*. This is the oldest tree on the island and very impressive to see. A hiking route has been set out through the fairytale forests that takes about half an hour. During this walk you also have the possibility to enjoy a picnic, or something to drink (bring your own). This hike is not suitable for wheelchairs or baby strollers.

Hòfi Pastor → Christoffel Park
From Hòfi Pastor you continue the Weg naar Westpunt. After about ten minutes you'll see signs for Christoffel Park.

On the right side of the Weg naar Westpunt is a parking lot and an office. Here you can pay for the entrance to the Christoffel Park and buy a map.

Christoffel Park

The park has one main road that runs in a large loop and ends at the entrance. Along the main road there are several parking places to stop and take a walk through the park.

You can of course go hiking through the park, but you can also book a jeep safari. On the way you'll get to hear a lot about all the flora and fauna in the park. For the more active traveler, there's also the possibility to climb the Christoffel Mountain. For more information about Christoffel Park, see page 59.

Christoffel Park → Shete Boka Park
Once you leave Christoffel Park continue on the Weg naar Westpunt.

After only a few minutes you'll see signs on the right side of the road for National Park Shete Boka.

Shete Boka Park

Although you can choose to leave your car in the main parking lot and take a walk along the bokas (inlets), this is not recommended: the distances between the bokas are quite big and limestone plains get hot in the middle of the day.

The best way to see the different bokas is by car: you can park your car at every boka, and then explore it on foot.

Tip: preferably visit the Shete Boka Park on a day with lots of wind, this makes it even more spectacular! See also page 61.

Landhuis Knip

Landhuis Knip is a historic building near the most western point of Curaçao. The mansion owes its fame to the slave revolt that started in 1795 from the plantations at Knip.

Tula is the person who led the slave revolt and he is still remembered by many as a hero. The mansion houses a museum, which revolves around Tula. See also page 74.

Landhuis Knip → Playa Abao (Grote Knip)
From Landhuis Knip follow the signs to Playa Abao.

Playa Abao is at the end of the road that leads through the plantations at Knip. At the beginning of this road you can also turn left at the T-junction, you will arrive at a very small beach, called Kleine Knip.

Finally, continue on the main road to head back to Willemstad. Via the Weg naar Sta. Cruz you'll end up on the Weg naar Westpunt. Follow the signs for Willemstad.

Playa Abao (Grote Knip)

Playa Abao is part of the plantations that belong to Knip. The beach is therefore also called 'Knip', or 'Kenepa', named after fruit produced by the Kenepa tree that grows in this area. After the strenuous activities of the day, it's wonderful to have a snack at Playa Abao and take a refreshing dip. See also page 45.

CHILL
SURF
S.U.P.
FOOd
dRiNKS
SWiM

2
Route 2
The unexpected
east
RELAX

Westpunt
Weg naar Westpunt
CHRISTOFFEL PARK
Lagun
Jan Donker
Barber
Soto
Weg naar Santa Cruz
Tera Korá
Weg naar Westpunt
HATO A
Jan Kok
Sint Willibrordus
Grote Berg
Weg naar Westpunt
Jan Kok Baai
Bullenbaai
Weg naar Bullenbaai
Sint Michiel
Blauwbaai

Route 2

Open this route in
Google Maps
Alöe Vera Plantation
Chichi Curaçao
Number Ten
4 Ostrich Farm
Restaurant Zambezi
5 Sint Jorisbaai
Santa
Catarina
Brievengat
Bonamweg
Weg naar Santa Catarina
Gosieweg
Franklin D. Rooseveltweg
Winston Churchillweg
Ring
Santa Rosaweg
Santa
Rosa
Ring
Sint Jorisbaai
Seru Loraweg
Weg naar Fuik
WILLEMSTAD
Piscaderabaai
Schottegat
Piscadera
Ring
Saliña
Lagun
Jan Thiel
Spaanse
Water
Oostpunt
Otrobanda
Punda
Pietermaal
Jan Thiel
Caracasbaai
Santa
Barbara
2 Tugboat
1 Curaçao Sea Aquarium
3 Landhuis Bloemhof
PORT

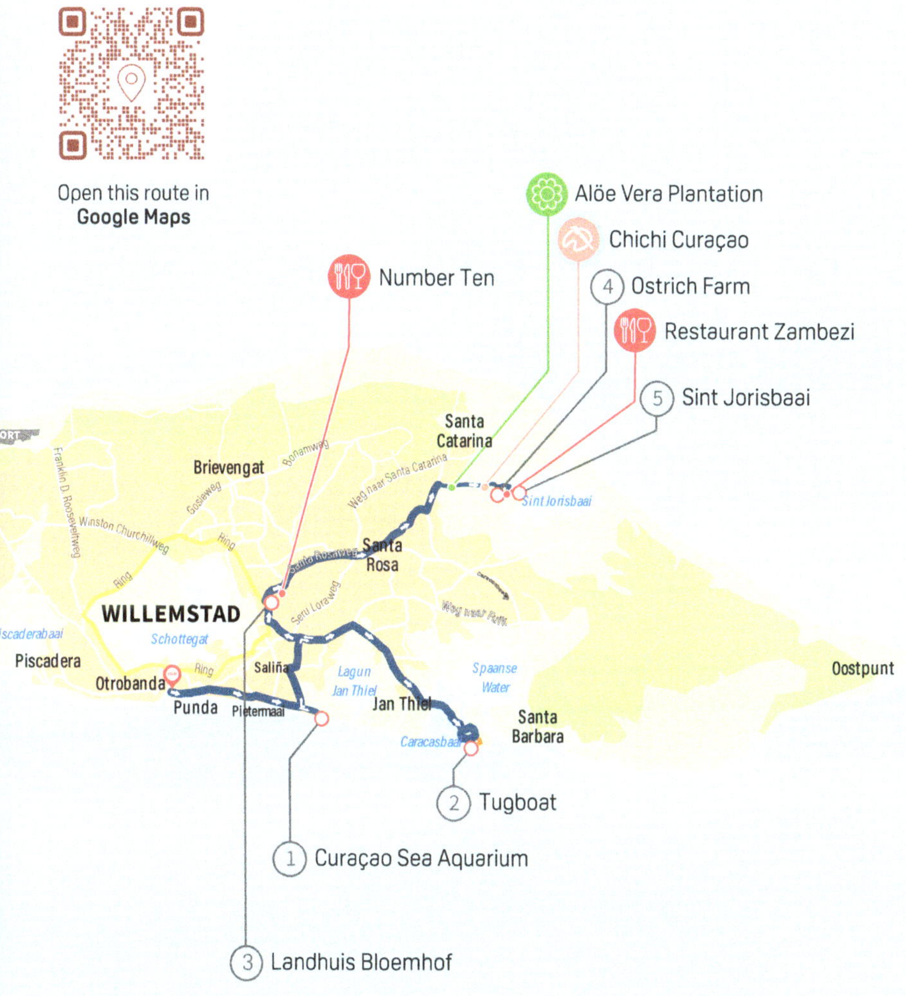

The unexpected east of Curaçao

The east side of Curaçao is a place with many contrasts. Whereas the immediate surroundings of Willemstad are fully developed, just a few miles away, you'll encounter fewer and fewer houses. More towards the north-east the area even looks a bit like Texas: dry, desolate and an occasional stray dog. The most expensive resorts and villa parks are also located on the east side of the island.

This route shows you the surprising contrasts on the east side of the island, fun for both young and old. Don't forget to bring your snorkel set.

About this route

We start the route in Willemstad. At the top of each page you can find the directions, with an indication of the duration of the route. This route takes a full day, but can be cut short, if desired, by skipping certain parts

Using Google Maps offline

If you have a Wi-Fi connection, you can download the map of Curaçao on Google Maps. Scan the QR code on the previous page while on Wi-Fi and this route will automatically open in Google Maps. If you turn on GPS along the way, you can navigate the island without an internet connection for free.

START

🚗
10
min

Willemstad → Curaçao Sea Aquarium
From Punda drive out of Willemstad via the Pietermaai street and
Penstraat. Continue on this road along the coast.

At the end of this road you'll arrive at the car park for the Sea Aquarium
Park Curaçao, where you can park your car (paid parking).

Curaçao Sea Aquarium

The Curaçao Sea Aquarium is a tourist attraction and an absolute must for
any vacationer on the island. The various aquariums are home to a variety of
(underwater) animals from around Curaçao. Get to know the underwater world
of the Caribbean in a fun way.

It's much more fun to attend a number of training demonstrations with sea
lions or dolphins. You can also help with feeding the flamingos, for example.
Many people dream of swimming with dolphins. Reservations required. See
also page 69.

Curaçao Sea Aquarium → Tugboat
Drive back on the same road you took and after appr. 1/4 mile turn right in Koraalspechtweg.

Turn right at the end and then take an immediate left in the Dominguitoweg. At the end, turn right into the Caracasbaaiweg. At the roundabout all the way at the end of this road, turn left.

Approximately 150 feet before the end of this road, turn left and at the end turn right again. Drive left around the big house (bad road), and park at the Tugboat Beach Bar.

• Tugboat

The tugboat is a well-known snorkeling spot on Curaçao. You can go snorkeling or diving to a sunken tugboat. The boat is just below the water surface and is covered with coral. There are always many fish to be found here and it's a hot spot for snorkeling.

Be careful not to touch the boat, the coral that is on it can cause irritation, and the material is very fragile.

15
min

Tugboat → Landhuis Bloemhof
Drive back via the same road, and at the roundabout turn right back to the Caracasbaaiweg. After about 3.5 miles, take the second road on the roundabout at the Janwé church to the Saturnustraat. Take the fourth exit on the right, go right again at the end. A road map can be useful for this part of the route. After 500 yards turn left to the Mercuriusstraat. At the end turn right on the Schottegatweg Oost.

Keep right after 1/2 mile, in the bend you'll see Landhuis Bloemhof. 100 Yards past Landhuis Bloemhof is restaurant Number Ten, a great lunch spot.

Landhuis Bloemhof

This mansion dates back to 1735 and is beautifully preserved. It is home to a rich world of art, culture and nature. Follow the various paths through the garden and admire the various works of art by changing artists with the highlight being the Cathedral of thorns (see photo below).

The plot is three acres in size and can be visited either independently or with a guide. Visit bloemhof.cw for current tours. Admission to the mansion is NAF 18.- for adults and NAF 10.50 for children. Open Mondays through Saturdays from 9am to 2pm.

Landhuis Bloemhof→ Ostrich Farm
Turn right on the Santa Rosaweg and follow this street for 4 miles to the end. Turn left to the Kaminda Mitologia. After 1/2 mile turn right and follow the sign to the Ostrich & Game Farm. Eat or drink something at the Zambezi Restaurant.

15 min

Ostrich Farm

Ostriches on a tropical island like Curaçao? The Ostrich Farm shows that this is a great concept. Every hour a safari truck leaves for a tour along the ostrich fields. During the tour you can get to know these peculiar animals in a fun way.

During a visit to the Ostrich Farm, you'll be feeling like you've briefly left Curaçao. The surroundings sooner resemble the nature of Africa. See also page 71.

An alternative to the Ostrich Farm is the nearby Aloe Vera Plantation, here you can learn everything about this plant and its medicinal effects.

Ostrich Farm → Sint Jorisbaai
Turn right when leaving the parking and continue the road till the end and you will arrive at Sint Jorisbaai.

3 min

To drive back from Sint Jorisbaai to Willemstad, head back and turn left at the main road. At the end of this road you turn right at the Weg naar Montana and follow signs for Willemstad.

Sint Jorisbaai

A few hundred yards past the Ostrich Farm is St. Joris Baai. It's a good kitesurfing spot. A spectacular sport to watch, or to try out yourself.

If you want to give it a try it is wise to arrange a lesson. See also page 67.

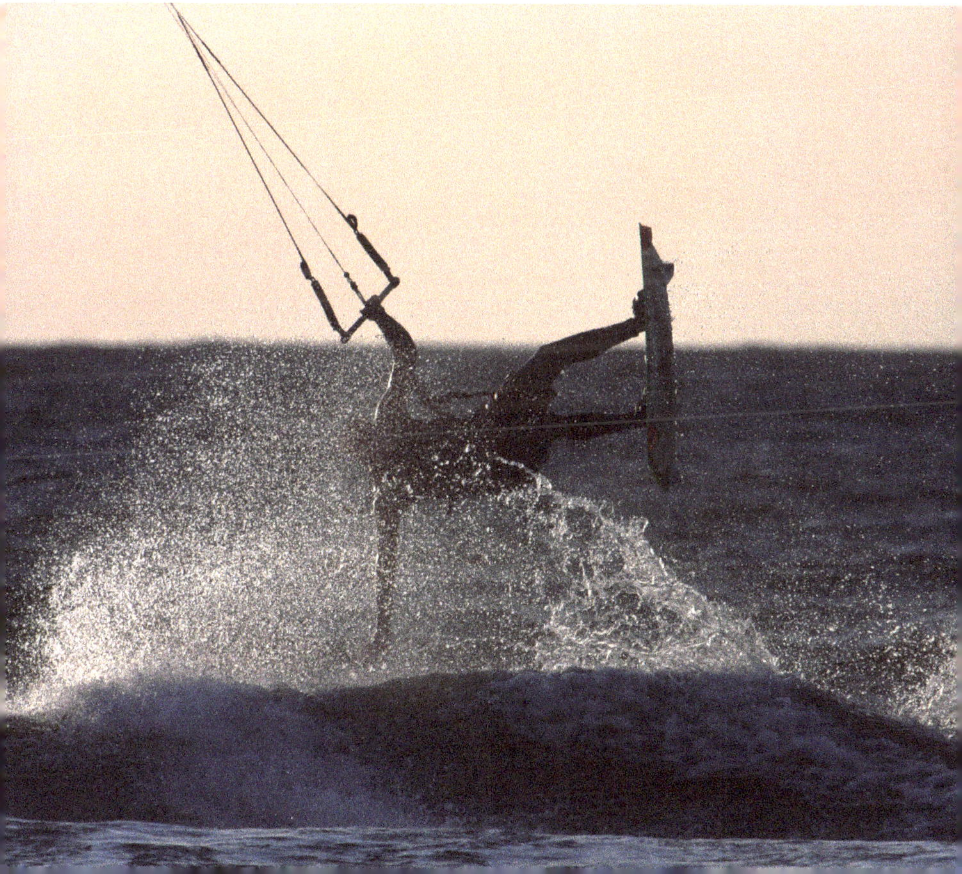

ster naar PARADISE FM
stem af op 103.1
zen KCC 7830 km
Breda
HOEKTRANS
Kapperie
ster 90 66 KM
FRENZZ
BAR & HAPAS
VE YOUR BOX WORLDWIDE
7830 Km
w mybw.nl
n Catering
OASIA 5,4 KM
cycling curaçao

Practical information

Practical information

Can I connect my telephone charger to a power socket in Curaçao? What should I do if I have a car accident? What currency do they use on Curaçao? Can I just pay with my credit card? Where can I find the best supermarkets and when are they open?

You'll find an answer to these and other practical questions in this chapter.

Language: learn some Papiamento!

Although the locals mostly speak Papiamento, almost everyone speaks Dutch and/ or English, but it is highly appreciated if you, as a visitor, can speak a few words of Papiamento.

The signage on Curaçao is always in Dutch. Many signs have been placed along the roads in recent years to indicate the routes to beaches, restaurants and other places of interest. Menus are always in Dutch or English.

Papiamentu evolved over centuries from several African languages, supplemented by words from Portuguese, Spanish, English and Dutch. As mentioned, it is much appreciated by the locals if you speak a few words of Papiamentu as a guest. Therefore, we provide a list of common words.

List of words

English	Papiamento	English	Papiamento
Welcome	Bon bini	Pharmacy	Botica
Good morning.	Bon dia	House	Kas
Good afternoon,	Bon tardi	Map	Mapa
Good evening	Bon nochi	Suitcase	Falis
Bye!	Ayo!	Police	Polis
		Check	Kuenta
How's everything going?	Kon ta bai?	Beach	Playa
		Hill/mountain	Seru
All is well!	Mi ta bon		
Thank you	Danki	One	Un
You're welcome	Di nada	Two	Dos
		Three	Tres
Yes	Si	Four	Kuater
No	Nò	Five	Sinku
Good	Bon	Six	Seis
Many	Hopi	Seven	Siete
Little	Tiki	Eight	Ocho
Please	Por fabor	Nine	Nuebe
Where is... ?	Unda ta...	Ten	Dies
Excuse me	Despensa	Hundred	Cien
Very nice	Hopi dushi		

Transport on Curaçao

Public transport

There are several bus lines on Curaçao and there are also minibuses around. The large bus lines run on fixed routes and don't deviate, but usually only run once an hour or sometimes even less. The minibuses don't run according to fixed times, but due to the large number of minibuses you never have to wait long.

The route the minibuses take is indicated with a sign behind the windshield and they can be recognized by the word *'BUS'* on the license plate. One of the advantages of these minibuses is that the drivers - sometimes for a small fee – can deviate from the route and drop you off somewhere. Payment is made in cash to the driver, a ride of about 20 minutes costs a few Antillean guilders.

There are two bus stations in Willemstad. One is in the Punda district, the other in Otrobanda. You can go to the bus station in Otrobanda to see the departure times of the big bus lines.

From Punda the buses leave in the eastern direction of the island. Most tourist areas such as Mambo Beach Boulevard and Jan Thiel are easily accessible from Willemstad by public transport. Keep in mind that after ten o'clock in the evening there's no more public transport on the island!

The Otrobanda district is to the west side of the island. The minibuses only have short routes here, while the big buses run all the way to Westpunt. The disadvantage is that most of the beaches are a few miles away from the main road (at least half an hour's walk). Therefore public transport is less suitable to discover the west side of Curaçao.

Taxis

There are plenty of taxis available on Curaçao. There are taxi stands at the airport, in Willemstad, at many hotels and at the nightlife hubs. Not all taxis run on a meter, but run according to fixed rates. From the airport to Willemstad (Otrobanda) you pay an average of NAF 80 (about $ 50). You pay about NAF 90 to Mambo Beach Boulevard and about NAF 100 to Jan Thiel. You can recognize official taxis by checking the number plate which starts with *TX*.

Rental cars

Although Curaçao offers some opportunities to find your way around the island with the help of public transport and taxis, you really need your own transport to truly explore the island. There are several well-known car rental companies at the airport, which generally offer a well-maintained fleet of vehicles.

Important!

It is advisable to ask for the most important traffic rules when renting a car, these differ slightly from the American and European traffic regulations. In case of wet road surfaces, pay extra attention, because the roads can be very slippery due to oil residue!

          PRACTICAL INFORMATION

Below you'll find some of the most important traffic rules:
- At T-junctions, a driver on the road that ends must yield the right of way to drivers on the through road.
- Drivers of motor vehicles have the right of way over other road users (including mopeds), except when they cross other road users when turning.
- The right of way rules at roundabouts vary. Pay close attention to the signs and markings on the road surface, although sometimes these are also poorly visible because they have been worn away. Pay close attention to other traffic before deciding who has the right of way.
- On Curaçao, people do not always follow the rules, so always pay attention at intersections.

Especially towards Westpunt, the road surface of some roads is poor, with potholes here and there.

Money on Curaçao

The guilder

The local currency on Curaçao is the Dutch-Antillean Florin (NAF), also called the Antillean Dutch Guilder (ANG). The exchange rate of the Antillean guilder is linked to the US dollar at a fixed exchange rate. This price is set at $ 1 is NAF 1.78. In many places it's also possible to pay with US dollars, as they circulate freely.

ATMs

On Curaçao there are plenty of banks and ATMs where you can withdraw money in local curreny or in US dollars. For this, depending on the bank, a surcharge can be charged. It's also possible to pay with your credit card all over the island.

Supermarkets

The supermarkets on Curaçao are influenced by both the Dutch and the American market. You can see these influences in the range and quantity of products and goods, but also in the design and appearance of the store. Most supermarkets are pretty large and they also sell many non-food items. Most products are imported from America and Europe. Most vegetables and fruit is imported from South America.

The following supermarkets are the best choice for holidaymakers due to their location, wide range and quality of products:

Centrum Supermarket, two stores:
1. Weg naar Bullenbaai, next to Piscadera just west of Willemstad.
   Open: Mon - Sat 7:30am - 8pm, Sun 7:30am - 6pm
2. SBN Doormanweg, Mahaai, ten oosten van Willemstad.
   Open: Mon - Sat 7:30am - 8pm, Sun 7:30am - 6pm

Van den Tweel, two stores:
1. Kaya Adriatiko, Jan Thiel. Open: daily 7:30am - 9pm
2. Kaya Jacob Posner 28, Zeelandia, just north east of Willemstad.
   Open: daily 7:30am - 8:30pm

Apart from *Centrum* and *Van den Tweel*, the supermarkets *Vreugdenhil* and *Best Buy* are also recommended. Most supermarkets can be found in the surroundings of Willemstad, in the direction of Westpunt you'll find just a few small stores.

Drinking water & electricity

On Curaçao, the seawater is purified using a unique and costly process. The result is excellent drinkable tap water, known as the cleanest water in the Caribbean.

Because desalinating the seawater is a very costly process, the tariffs for water consumption are considerably higher than in the USA. Using water economically is therefore a must in Curaçao and par for the course.

Electricity

The default grid voltage on Curaçao is 110-130 volts/50Hz and the default plug type is a two-pin 'Type A' power plug, as used in the USA. There are however appartments and hotels which provide European power outlets, using 220 volts and requiring a European plug. Plug adaptors can be bought in the centre of Willemstad.

However most electrical appliances like phone chargers and notebooks are compatible with 110-230 volts, always check the compatibility of your appliances before plugging in.

Renewable energy

Curaçao still has insufficient options for running the electricity grid on green energy. In the nineties, two wind farms were installed along the north coast to generate energy. These wind turbines, however, were unable to withstand the strong winds and the salt coming from the sea, and they were therefore replaced a few years ago by new turbines. The parks are in the direction of Westpunt at *Tera Kora*, and slightly more to the east at *Playa Kanoa*.

Important phone numbers

Curaçao is equipped with an excellent mobile telephone network, which - with the exception of remote areas - offers network coverage throughout the entire island. Bringing a mobile phone is therefore always recommended in case of emergencies.

Curaçao has the following important telephone numbers:

Police / fire department: 911
Ambulance: 912
Coast guard: 913
Curaçao Road Service (in case of traffic accidents): 199

The international access number for Curaçao is +5999.

Traffic accident?

If you're involved in a traffic accident, it's good to know that you should always call Curaçao Road Service on 199 for assistance and help with any material damages, and not the police.

The Curaçao Road Service is the authority in Curaçao that draws up an official damage report, which must also be handed over to the insurance company. Without a damage report from Curaçao Road Service, the car rental company can recover the damages from you, because it is not covered by the insurance!

Index

www.ingramcontent.com/pod-product-compliance
Lightning Source LLC
Chambersburg PA
CBHW040141160726
48006CB00014B/1582